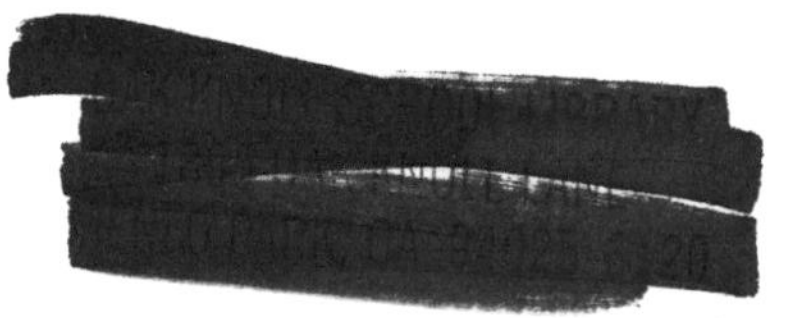

YOUNG SCIENTIST

THE AGE OF COMPUTERS

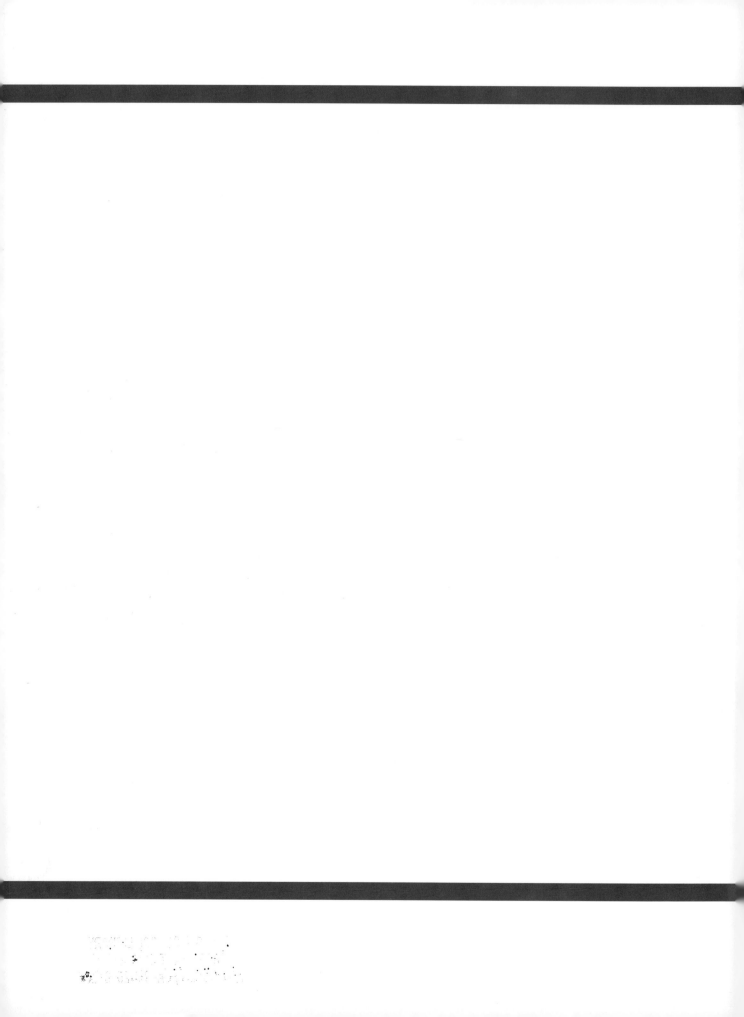

YOUNG SCIENTIST

THE AGE OF COMPUTERS

World Book, Inc.
a Scott Fetzer company
Chicago London Sydney Toronto

Activities that have this warning symbol require some adult supervision!

The quest to explore the known world and to describe its creation and subsequent development is nearly as old as mankind. In the Western world, the best-known creation story comes from the book of Genesis. It tells how God created the earth and all living things. Modern religious thinkers interpret the Biblical story of creation in various ways. Some believe that creation occurred exactly as Genesis describes it. Others think that God's method of creation is revealed through scientific investigation. *Young Scientist* presents an exciting picture of what scientists have learned about life and the universe.

World Book, Inc.
525 W. Monroe
Chicago, IL 60661

For information on other World Book products, call 1-800-255-1750.

ISBN: 0-7166-6304-X
Library of Congress Catalog Card No. 95-62167

Printed in Mexico

1 2 3 4 5 6 7 8 9 10 99 98 97 96

Acknowledgments

The publishers of **World Book's Young Scientist** acknowledge the following photographers, publishers, agencies, and corporations for photographs used in this volume. All entries marked with an asterisk (*) denote photographs created exclusively for **World Book's Young Scientist.**

Cover	Front: Blair Seitz, Photo Researchers; Brownie Harris, The Stock Market; Nelson Morris/SS from Photo Researchers; Paul Barton, The Stock Market; Jeremy Burgess/SPL from Photo Researchers; Jeff Guerrant*; Peter Menzel
	Back: Bob Daemmrich
8/9	Hank Morgan, Science Photo Library; Spectrum Colour Library; ZEFA Picture Library
12/13	Sarah Errington, Hutchison Library
24/25	Tim Defrisc, Allsport Photographic
28/29	David Higgs, Tony Stone Worldwide
32/33	Nelson Morris, Science Photo Library; Andrew Syred/SPL from Photo Researchers
36/37	Jeff Guerrant*
40/41	James D. Wilson, Woodfin Camp, Inc; Hank Morgan/SS from Photo Researchers; Jeff Guerrant*
44/45	Jeff Guerrant*
50/51	Jeff Guerrant*
52/53	World Book photo
54/55	Paul Barton, The Stock Market; Tony Stone Worldwide; Peter Menzel
56/57	Tom Sheppard, Tony Stone Worldwide
58/59	ZEFA Picture Library; Shahn Kermani, Gamma/Liaison
60/61	Hank Morgan, Rainbow*

Illustrated by

Hemesh Alles
Sue Barclay
Richard Berridge
Bristol Illustrators
Marie DeJohn
Farley, White and Veal
Peter Geissler
Jeremy Gower
Kathie Kelleher
John Lobban
Louise Martin
Eileen Mueller Neill
Jeremy Pyke
Don Simpson
Gary Slater
Pat Tourret
Peter Visscher
Matthew White
Lynne Willey

Contents

MULTIPLAN
POUR
MACINTOSH
LE BASIC
MICROSOFT SUR
MACINTOSH

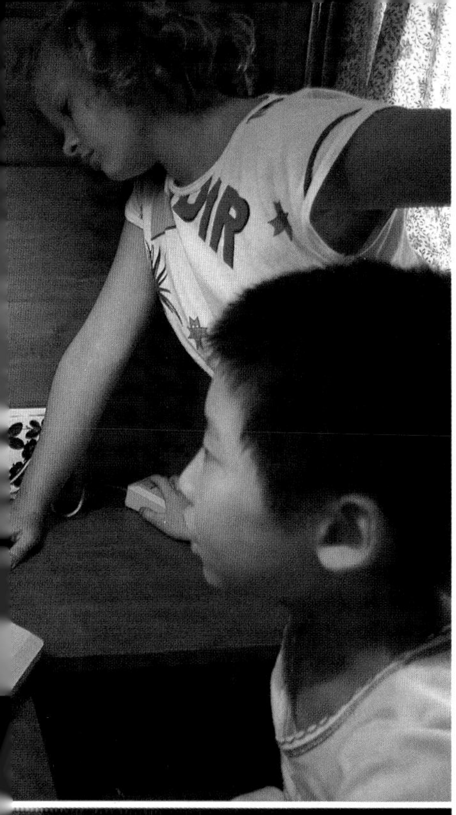

Why we need computers

Every day of your life you use a kind of computer— your brain. Your brain signals that you are hungry. It helps you to move, to work, and to remember things.

Our brains can also solve complicated mathematical problems, or **calculations.** But sometimes we need to calculate far more quickly than our brains can manage— and be sure that the answer is correct. This is when we need computers, which can solve problems and carry out the most difficult calculations with amazing speed and accuracy.

Computers are especially useful for storing a lot of information. They can keep words, pictures, and sounds in their memory and give you the information you need within seconds.

Even the most advanced computers are often easy to use. They communicate with you by flashing messages or pictures onto a screen, or sometimes they talk to you. You can play games with them, too.

Information at your fingertips

Your television can become a useful link with computers far away. You can find out all sorts of information just by pressing buttons on an electronic control panel at home. The information appears instantly on your television screen. You can find out the news, the weather forecast, sports results, and travel timetables. You can look at thousands of pages of information!

Computers make our lives easier in many ways— our cars travel more safely, our telephones work more quickly, businesses and banks operate more efficiently. Space travel would be impossible without computers.

Computers are useful for storing information and helping children with their studies. They are found at home and in the classroom.

Why do we count?

Can you imagine a time when people did not use numbers? The first people on earth lived by hunting wild animals and collecting wild fruit and nuts. They had no need to count. Numbers did not matter to them.

But then, about 11,000 years ago, herdsmen began to keep flocks of sheep and goats. They had to be able to count so that they would know if any of their animals were missing. The first calculations were made by counting in ones—'1 and 1 and 1,' and so on.

This method of counting is called **tallying.** One way herdsmen used to tally was to put a stone on a pile for each animal. Other ways were to tie knots in a length of rope, cut notches in sticks, or make scratches on a rock. Each stone, knot, notch, or scratch represented one sheep or goat.

About 11,000 years ago, the first farmers grew wheat, which they bundled into sheaves. Sheaves could be counted by tallying. The farmer might meet a herdsman who would exchange a goat for some wheat. How many sheaves of wheat would he exchange for an animal? Perhaps the herdsmen would hold up five fingers—five sheaves for a goat. Fingers provided a useful way of showing small numbers. But there was no way of writing numbers down or adding them together.

For each sheep, the shepherd puts one stone on the pile. Next time he counts them, he will take one stone off the pile for each sheep that he can see. If there are some stones left when he has finished counting, he will know that some animals are missing.

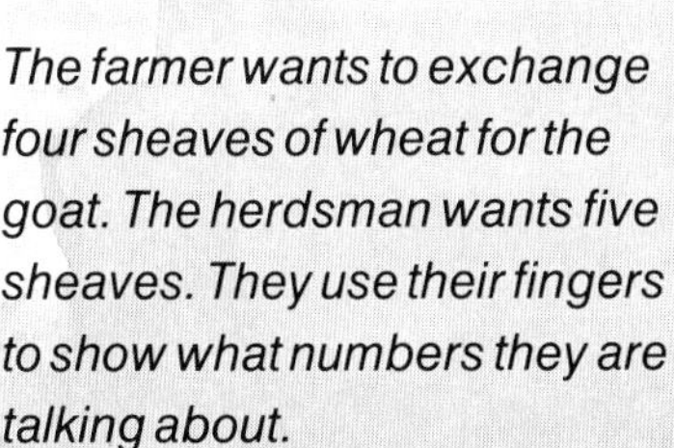

The farmer wants to exchange four sheaves of wheat for the goat. The herdsman wants five sheaves. They use their fingers to show what numbers they are talking about.

Can you tally?

You will need:

a large number of objects, such as marbles or coins

a long piece of string

a watch or clock

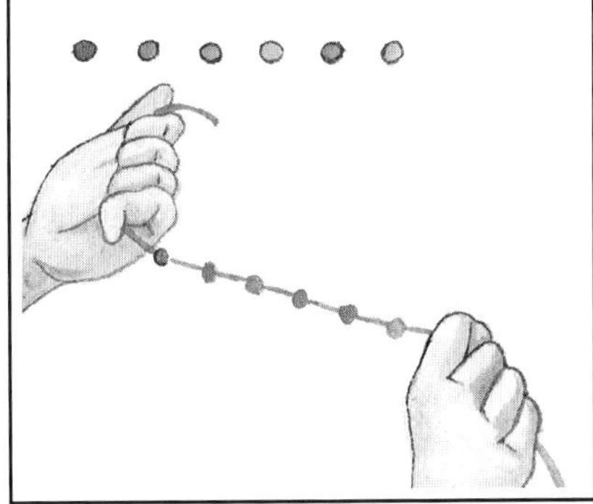

1. As you count each object, tie a knot in the string. Use a watch or clock to time yourself.

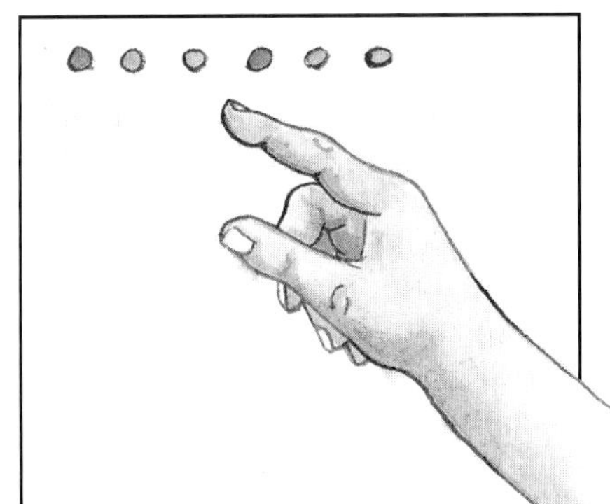

2. When you have finished, count the objects again in your usual way. Which method is faster?

Counting in tens

Do you ever count on your fingers? Our 10 fingers are useful for counting. Almost everyone in the world calculates using groups of 10. Even today, adults sometimes count on their fingers. We often use the word **digit** for each number. Digit comes from the Latin word *digitus*, meaning a finger.

When you count in tens, you are counting in what is called a **decimal system,** or **base 10.** The 10 digits used in base 10 are 0, 1, 2, 3, 4, 5, 6, 7, 8, 9. Every 10 ones, or **units,** make up one unit of a larger group. Ten ones make 10. Ten tens make 100, and so on. We show how many there are in each group by putting the figures in columns.

hundreds	tens	units
2	4	7

The number 247 means that there are two hundreds, four tens, and seven units.

The ***abacus*** *is a simple calculator that has been used for thousands of years. It is still used in some parts of the world today. Calculations are made by moving the beads along the wires.*

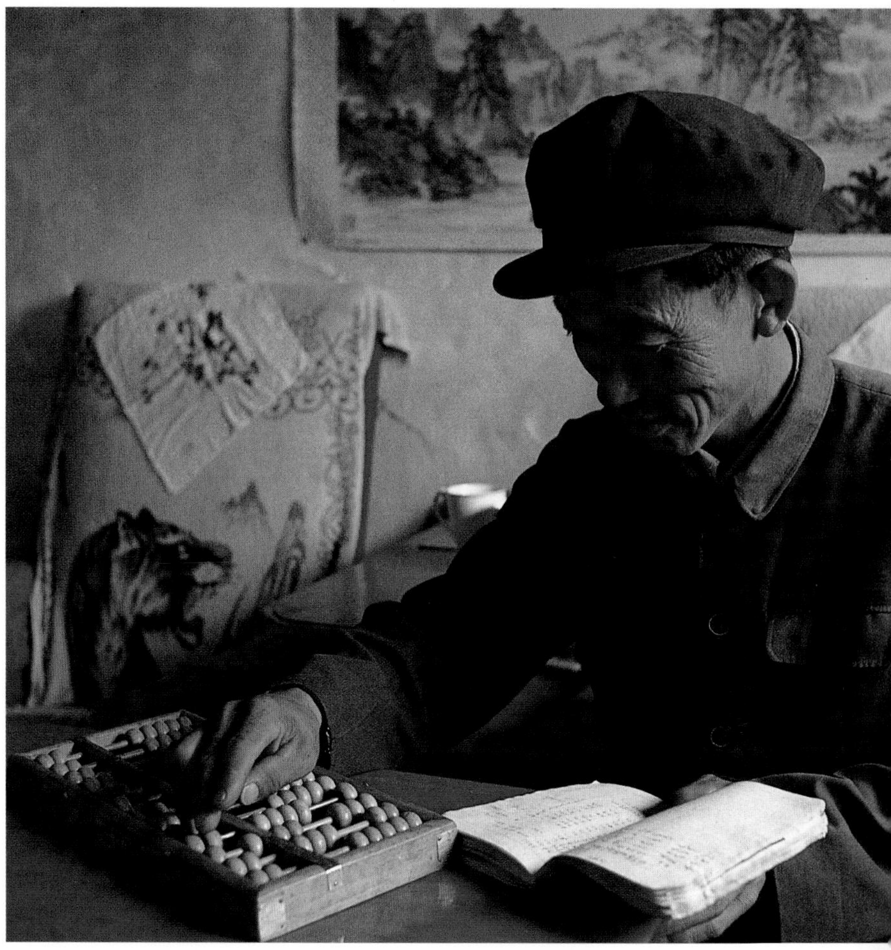

This Chinese farmer is using an abacus to work out his financial accounts.

Counting in twos

You don't have to count in tens. **Base 2,** called the **binary system,** uses only two digits, 0 and 1. Instead of columns of units, tens, and hundreds, base 2 uses columns of units, twos, fours, and so on. Each digit in a base 2 number is twice as much as the digit on its right. So the next column after fours would be eights (2×4). What would the column after this be? Look at the two tables and see how we write the numbers 0 to 8 in base 2— 9 and 10 are left for you to work out for yourself. How would the base 2 number 1011 be written in base 10?

Base 10		**Base 2**			
tens	**units**	**eights**	**fours**	**twos**	**units**
	0				0
	1				1
	2			1	0
	3			1	1
	4		1	0	0
	5		1	0	1
	6		1	1	0
	7		1	1	1
	8	1	0	0	0
	9				
1	0				

Base 2—the easy way

Here is an easy way to change base 2 numbers into base 10. Place your left hand on a sheet of paper with your palm facing down. With a pencil, trace your hand on the paper. Now write 16 on the little finger, 8 on the third finger, 4 on the middle finger, 2 on the first finger and 1 on the thumb.

Each finger stands for the digit 1 in base 2. So put a checkmark by each finger where there is a 1, and put a cross by it where there is a 0. Then add up the numbers beside all the checkmarks, and there's your answer. So 1011 looks like this.

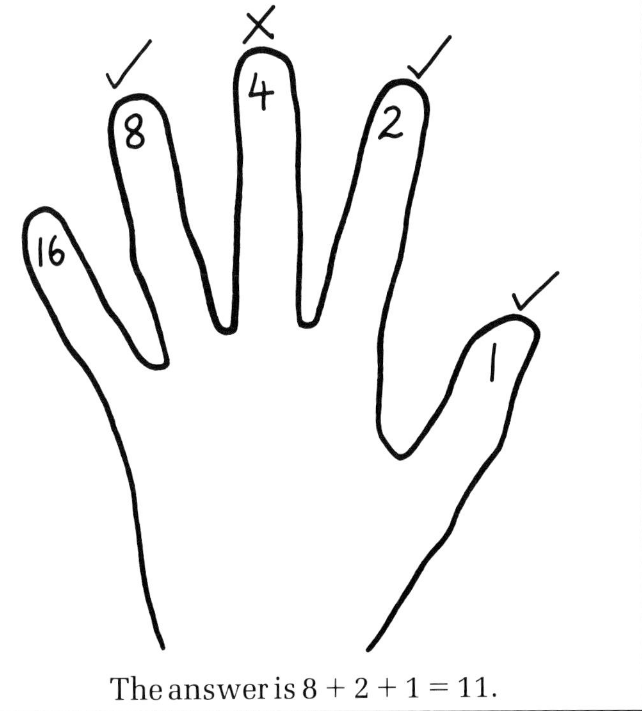

The answer is $8 + 2 + 1 = 11$.

Calculating

If we had plenty of time, we could make all the calculations we need by simply using **addition** or **subtraction.** This was what the first shepherds did with piles of stones. They placed one stone on the pile as they counted each sheep. Next time they counted, if there were any stones left over, they would know how many sheep were missing.

Each of these semitrailers can carry eight cars. How many cars are there altogether?

Multiplying sheep

It would be quicker to use one stone, for example, for every five sheep. At the end, the shepherd could count the stones and reckon five sheep for each stone. This is what we do when we use **multiplication.** We write down one number times another number. For example, four times five can be written as 4×5. If we want to work out how many legs a group of people have, we multiply the number of people by two because each person has two legs. If we want to work out the number of toes, we multiply the number of people by ten. This is much quicker than counting each leg or toe.

In the same way that a car is faster than a horse and cart, so can multiplication and division be a short-cut to many calculations.

Dividing a bag of candy

Division is another short-cut we use in calculation. If there is some candy to share among a group of children, one way of dividing it equally is to give each child one piece of candy, then another piece, and so on until there is no candy left. But if we know how much candy and how many children there are, it is quicker to work out the correct amount for each child and hand each one an equal amount of candy. If there are 21 candies and 7 children, we work out 21 divided by 7. We can write this as $21 \div 7$.

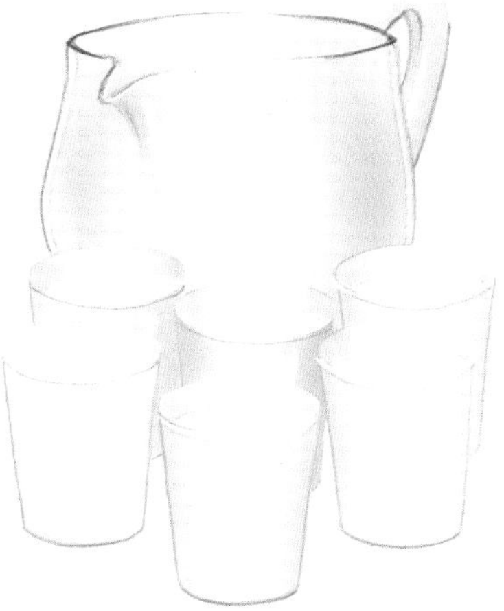

There are 36 children waiting at a lemonade stand to buy a drink. A one-quart (.95-liter) pitcher contains enough lemonade for six drinks. How many times must the pitcher be filled to serve all the children?

This bus can carry 40 passengers. There are 240 people who want to go to a football game. How many buses of this size will be needed?

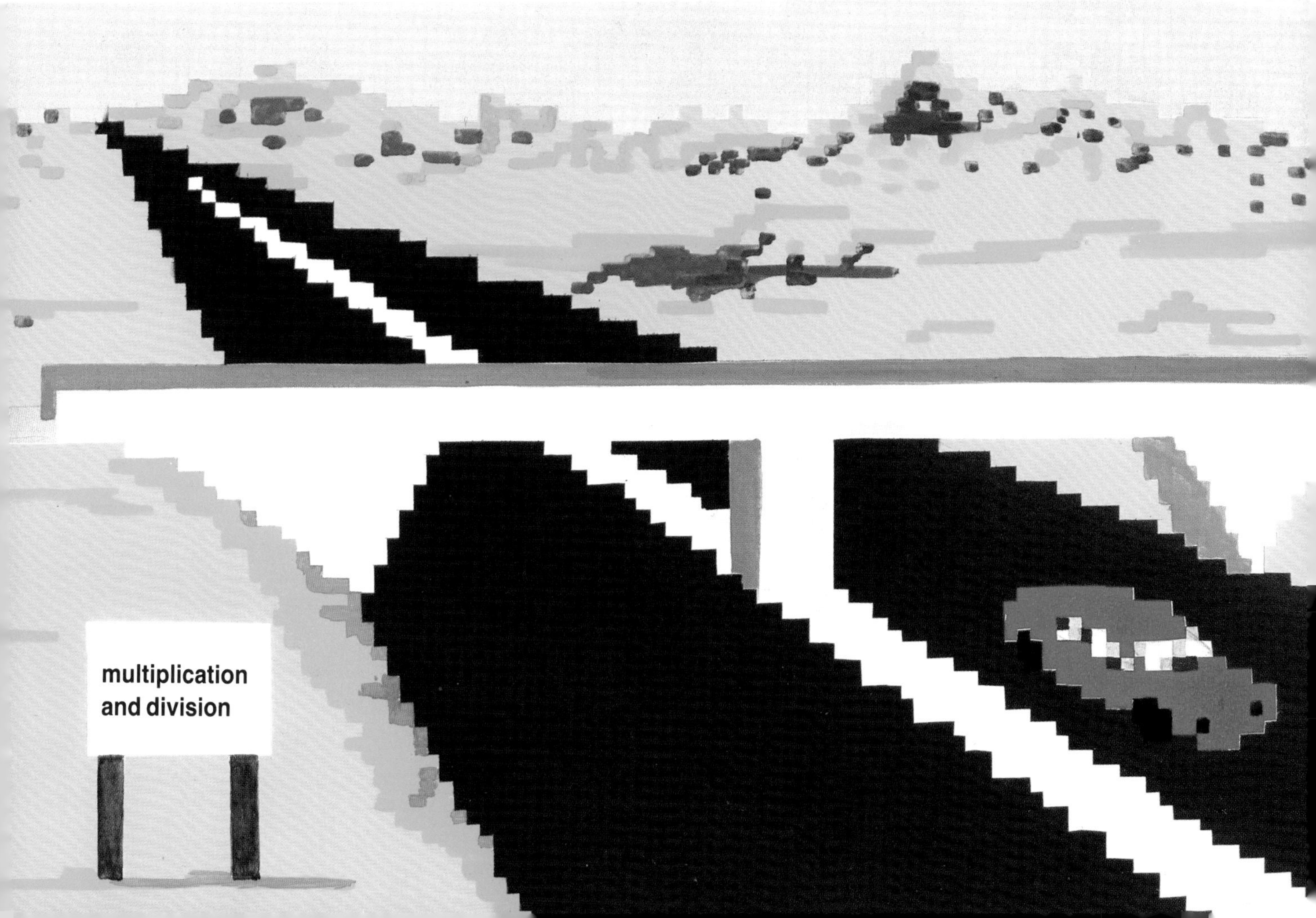

multiplication and division

Measurements

What would you use to weigh yourself or to measure the length of a piece of wood? In our homes, we have many different instruments for making measurements. There are rulers and tape measures for measuring **length.** In the kitchen, there is a cup or small pitcher with a scale for measuring the **volume** of liquids, such as water or milk. Scales and balances measure **weight,** and clocks and watches measure **time.** We use thermometers to measure **temperature.**

Measurements are made in units. Today, people in most countries—and all scientists—use the **metric system.** Metric units use base 10. In the United States, the **customary** or **English system** is used.

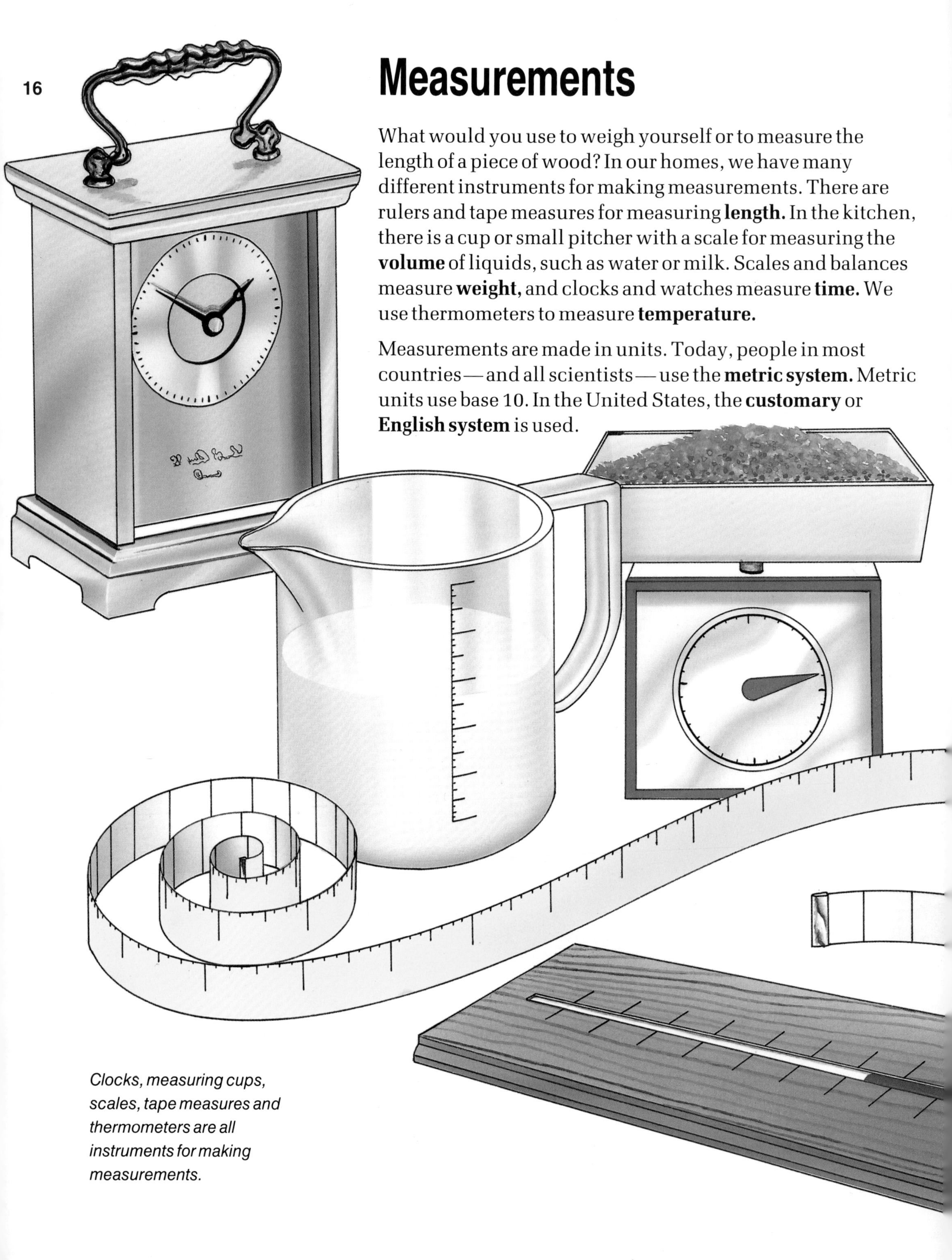

Clocks, measuring cups, scales, tape measures and thermometers are all instruments for making measurements.

Large and small

When we make calculations with measurements, we have to choose the best unit of measure. If you need to calculate the size of your room, you use feet and yards or meters. But if you want to find out the distance from Boston to San Diego, it is easier to use larger units, so you use miles or kilometers. In the same way, you would not use seconds to calculate how old you are, or years to time a race! An engineer who needs exact measurements for some special pieces of machinery calculates in units called microns, also known as micrometers. There are one million of these tiny units in one meter (1.1 yards).

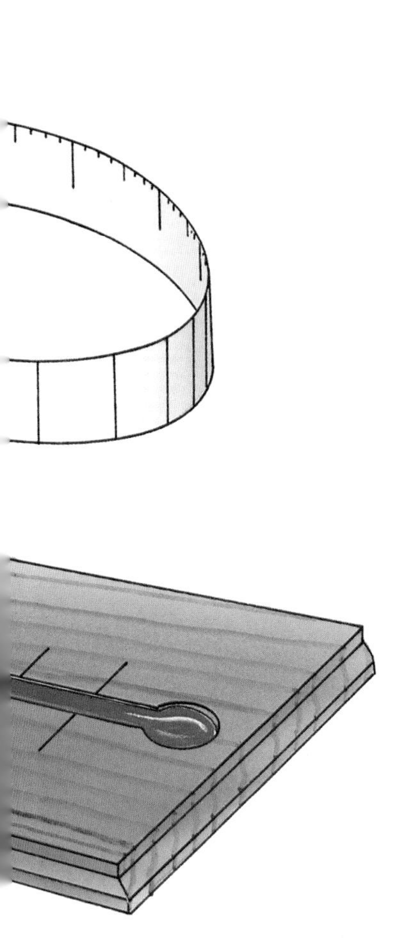

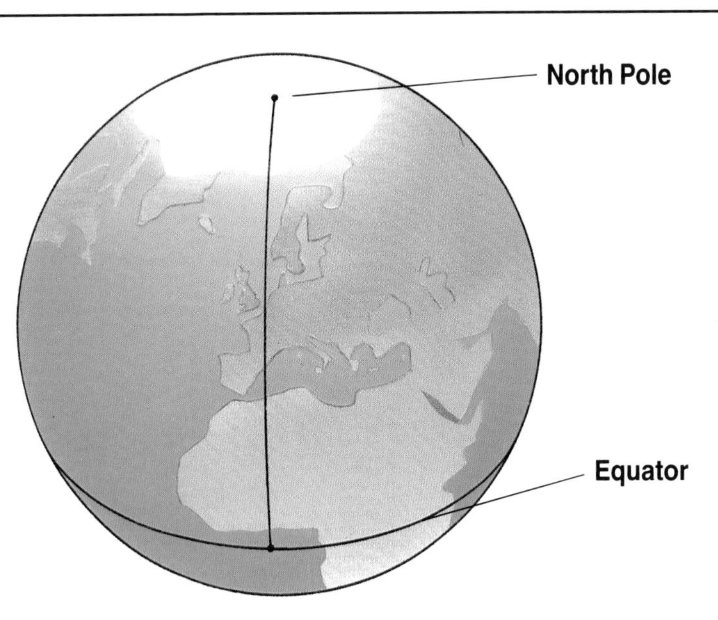

Finding the measure

The meter was first adopted in 1795. A group of French scientists calculated the length of a line from the North Pole to the equator, passing through Dunkerque, France, and Barcelona, Spain. They decided to divide this line into 10 million equal lengths—each length was called a meter.

Find out more by looking at pages **20–21**

Following the rules

Do we need to write down numbers in order to make calculations? No. We make calculations every day without using numbers at all.

What day of the week is it? You could answer that question by looking at the calendar. But you might work out that today is Tuesday because you remember that yesterday was Monday. Or you might realize that you have a music lesson today, and you always have music lessons on Tuesdays. Any of these three ways will give you the answer.

If you know it is Tuesday, you can also reckon that in three days you'll be able to watch your favorite TV program, because it is on Friday.

Reckoning and **reasoning** are other words for calculating. You ask a question, and you work out the answer. There can be only one correct answer. Either today is Tuesday, or it is not.

We learn to calculate by learning the rules and then by using or practicing them. The rules of calculation are based on reasoning, or **logic.** Whenever we work something out, we start with a question that has a YES or NO answer. Is it Tuesday? The answer is either YES (TRUE) or NO (FALSE, or NOT TRUE). Was yesterday Monday? If the answer to the first question is YES, then the answer to the second question must also be YES. The rule of the days of the week is that Tuesday comes after Monday.

These traffic lights are controlling two different streams of traffic. If you want to turn left, the green light says YES. If you want to go straight ahead, the red light says NO.

Asking questions

Do these cyclists want to go to Bigtown? If the answer is YES, they will need to take the road to the left. If it is NO, they will take the road to Littletown.

We ask ourselves questions with YES or NO answers many times every day. Can you open a locked door? If you have the right key, the answer is YES. If you haven't, NO. Is the light on? You don't have to look at the bulb. An electric switch gives an answer. If the switch is in the "on" position, the answer is YES. Traffic lights also give people YES or NO answers. Is it safe to walk across the road? A green light says YES. A red light says NO.

Find out more by looking at pages **18–19**

True or false?

Hans is a boy who lives in New City at 72 Temple Drive. He is 11 years old. Hans's sister, Elsa, is 8 years old. Hans and Elsa go to the same school. They have a dog called Max and a cat called Minni.

Is this a true story? Some of it may be true. Some may not. There may not even be a boy called Hans. We may be thinking of another boy called Fred or a girl called Margie. How can we tell if the story is true?

To find out, the story must be broken up into its parts. The YES or NO question we ask about each part is a **step** toward finding the correct answer. Is there someone called Hans? YES or NO. If YES, is the person a boy? YES or NO. If YES, does Hans live in New City? YES or NO. And so on.

Every question can be answered with a YES or NO. If one of the answers is NO, there is no need to ask any more questions. We know that the story isn't completely true.

You can think of these steps as pairs of **gates.** At each step, you can go through the YES gate or the NO gate. The YES gate takes you on to the next question. The NO gate stops you. It leads to a dead end.

You can write your own program with YES or NO questions on your computer at home or at school.

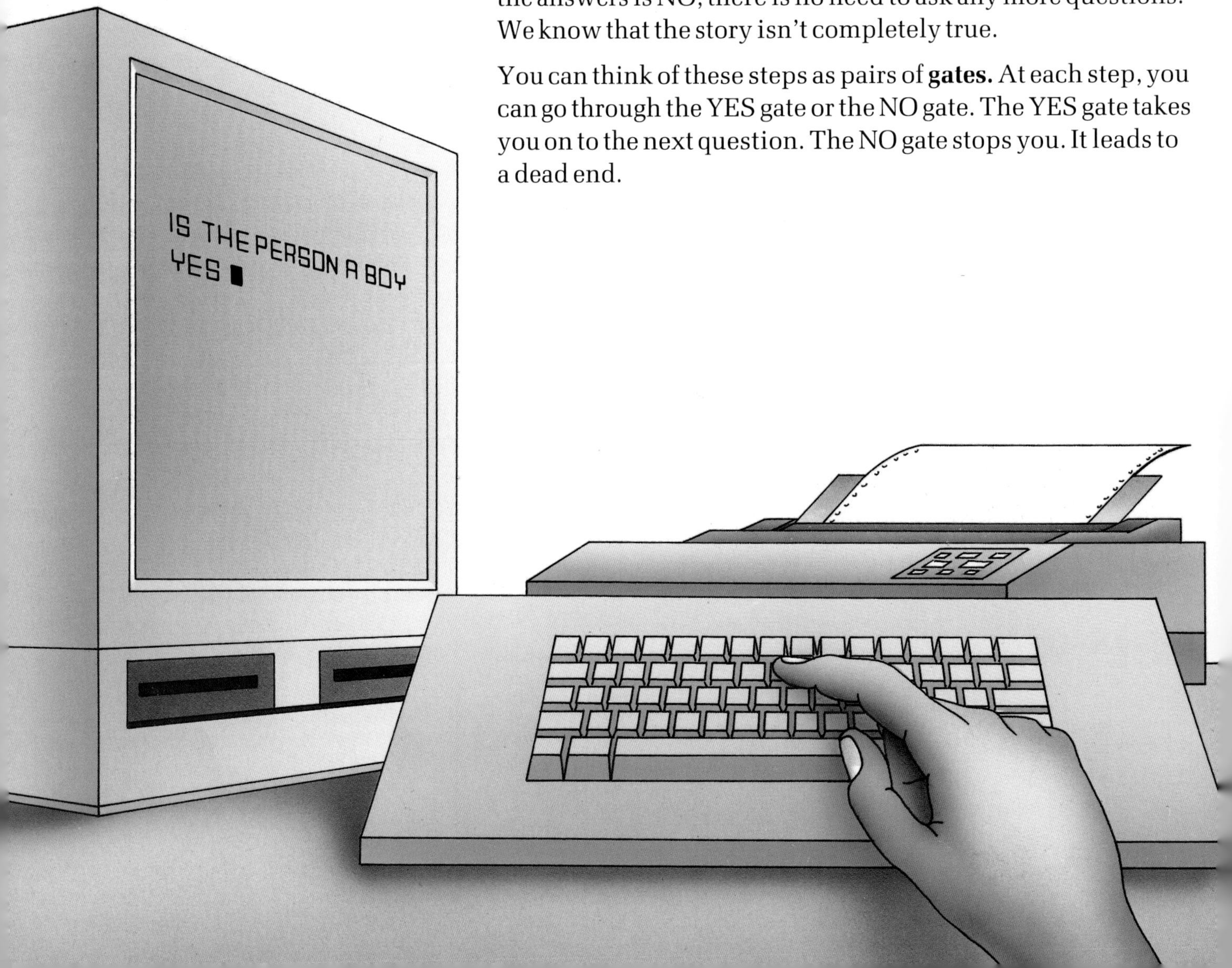

What is a maze?

These mazes are a collection of YES or NO gates. To find the way through them, you have to find all the YES gates. In the first maze on the right, it is easy to find the way. See how long it takes you to find your way through the other maze.

Here's another kind of maze. Two explorers discovered a strange animal living in a swamp. This four-legged animal had three eyes and a long tail. It had two horns and three spots down its back. The explorers couldn't agree what this strange creature was. One said it was a Cannotbe, the other thought it was a Neverwas. Can you go through this maze of information to find the answer?

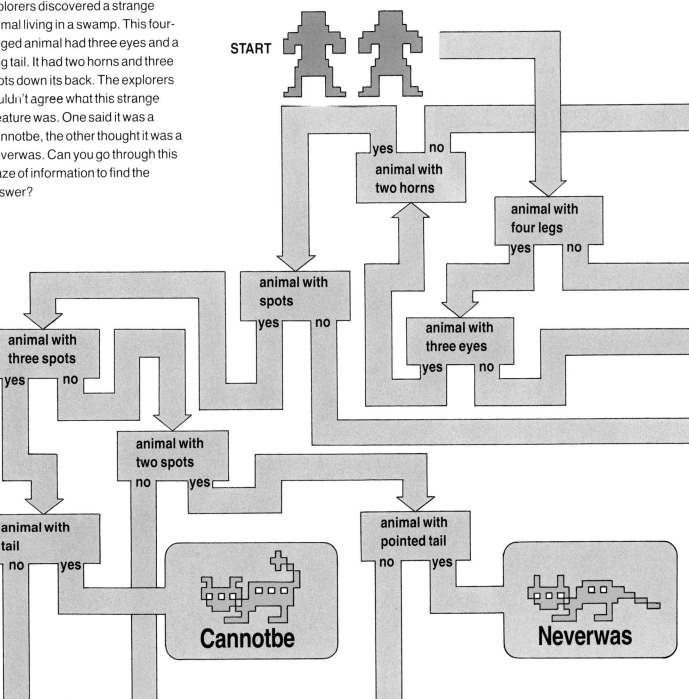

START

yes no
animal with two horns

animal with four legs
yes no

animal with spots
yes no

animal with three eyes
yes no

animal with three spots
yes no

animal with two spots
no yes

animal with tail
no yes

animal with pointed tail
no yes

Cannotbe

Neverwas

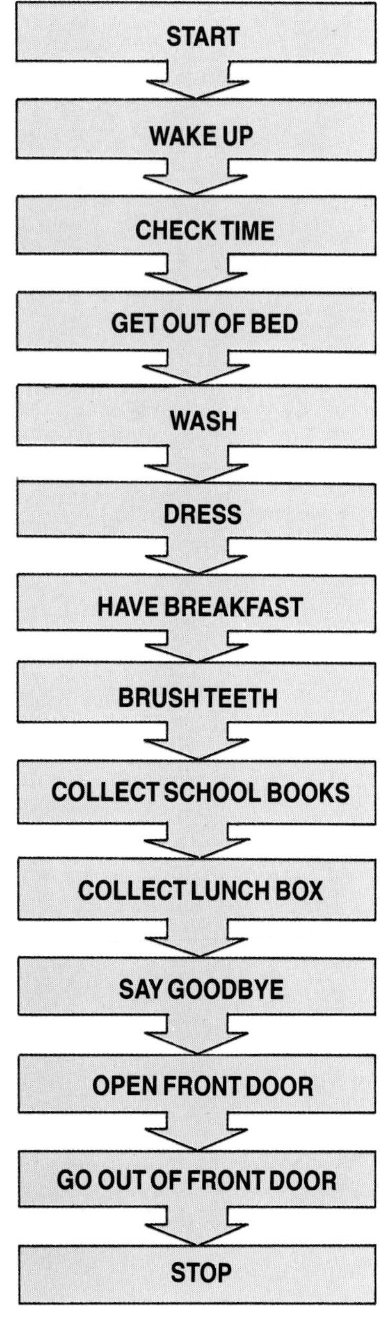

Step by step

When you wake up in the morning, you don't have to think about how to get ready for school. When you leave school at the end of the day, you don't have to think about how to go home. You have learned these things. They are stored in your memory.

When you get ready for school, you carry out a series of steps in a certain order. On the left, you can see a plan of the different steps that happen between waking up and going out of the door. This is called a **flow chart.** If you had never gotten ready for school before, you could follow the instructions in the flow chart. In the end, you would arrive on the front door step, ready for school.

On the right is a different flow chart showing how David goes home from school. It is called a **branch flow chart,** because there is a place in it where David has to choose between doing two things. Can you see where this choice happens?

Can you make a flow chart showing the steps that happen in making your bed or writing a letter? Here are the first two boxes of each chart to start you off.

Flow charts

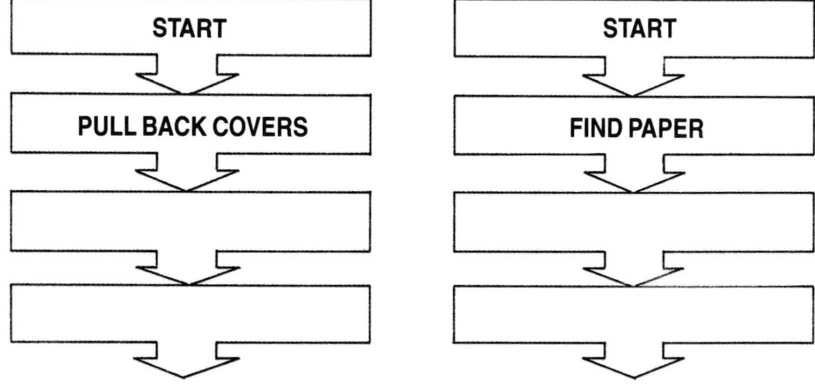

When you have completed these charts, try making a branch flow chart.

Show a choice about whether or not to use clean sheets, or whether to use a pencil or a pen to write the letter.

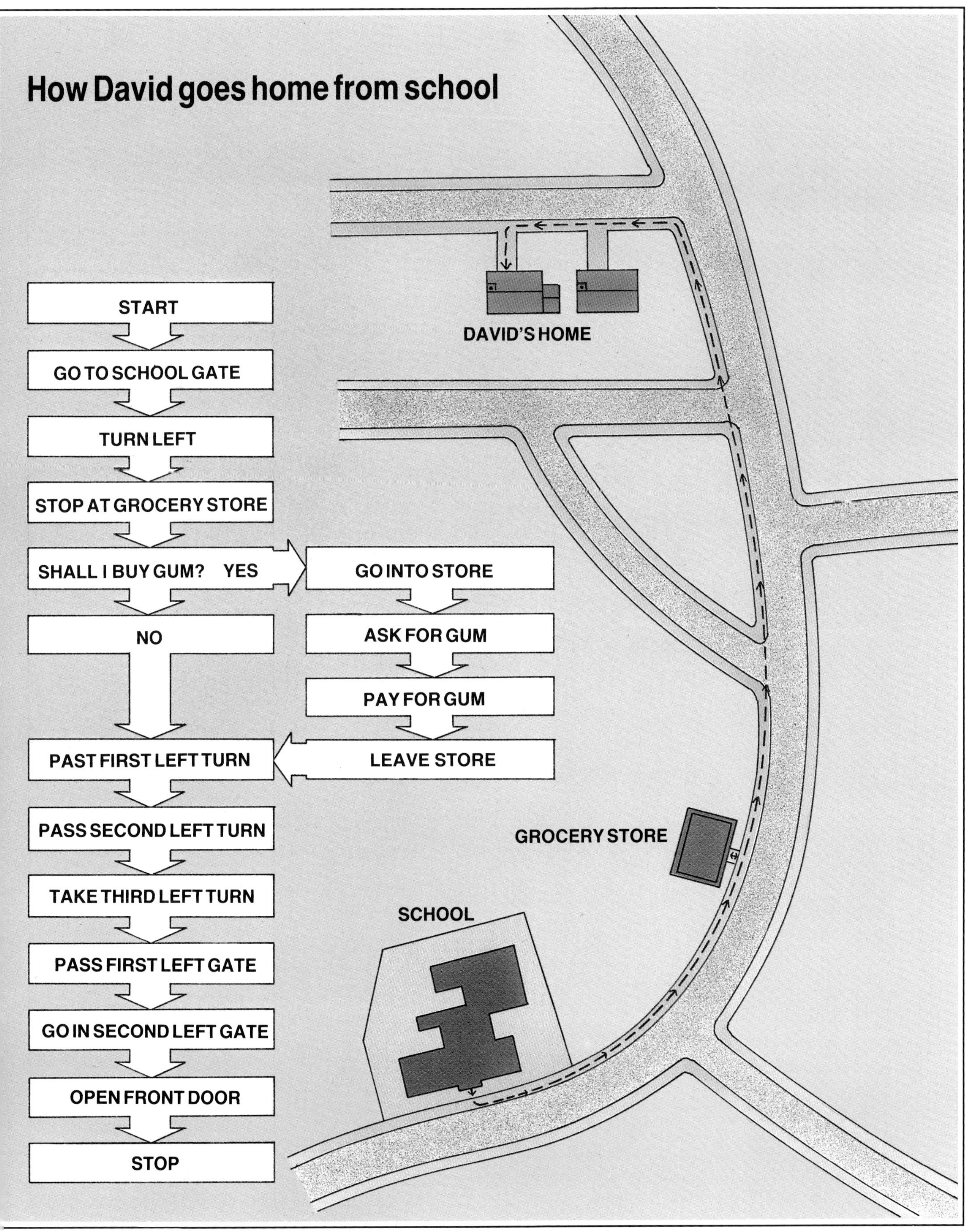
How David goes home from school
START
GO TO SCHOOL GATE
TURN LEFT
STOP AT GROCERY STORE
SHALL I BUY GUM? YES
GO INTO STORE
ASK FOR GUM
PAY FOR GUM
LEAVE STORE
NO
PAST FIRST LEFT TURN
PASS SECOND LEFT TURN
TAKE THIRD LEFT TURN
PASS FIRST LEFT GATE
GO IN SECOND LEFT GATE
OPEN FRONT DOOR
STOP
DAVID'S HOME
GROCERY STORE
SCHOOL

Find out more by looking at
pages **12–13**
14–15
22–23

What is a computer program?

When you play basketball, you throw the ball in the air. If it drops into the net, you have scored a goal. While throwing the ball, you made all sorts of calculations. Perhaps without realizing it, you calculated how far away the net was, how heavy the ball was, and how hard and at what angle you needed to throw it. With practice, you can make these calculations quickly and more accurately.

We all make calculations, either slowly or quickly. The quickest calculating machine of all is the **computer.**

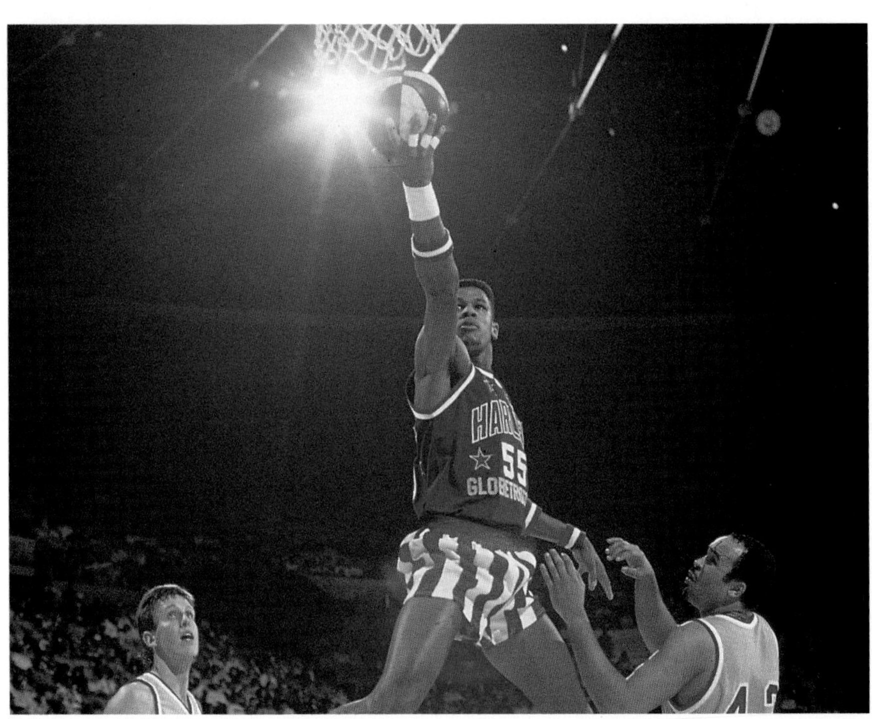

This player on the Harlem Globetrotters basketball team has to make very quick calculations in order to score a goal like this.

There are only two signals used in computer code—on and off. All the complicated calculations made by computers are based on just these two signals.

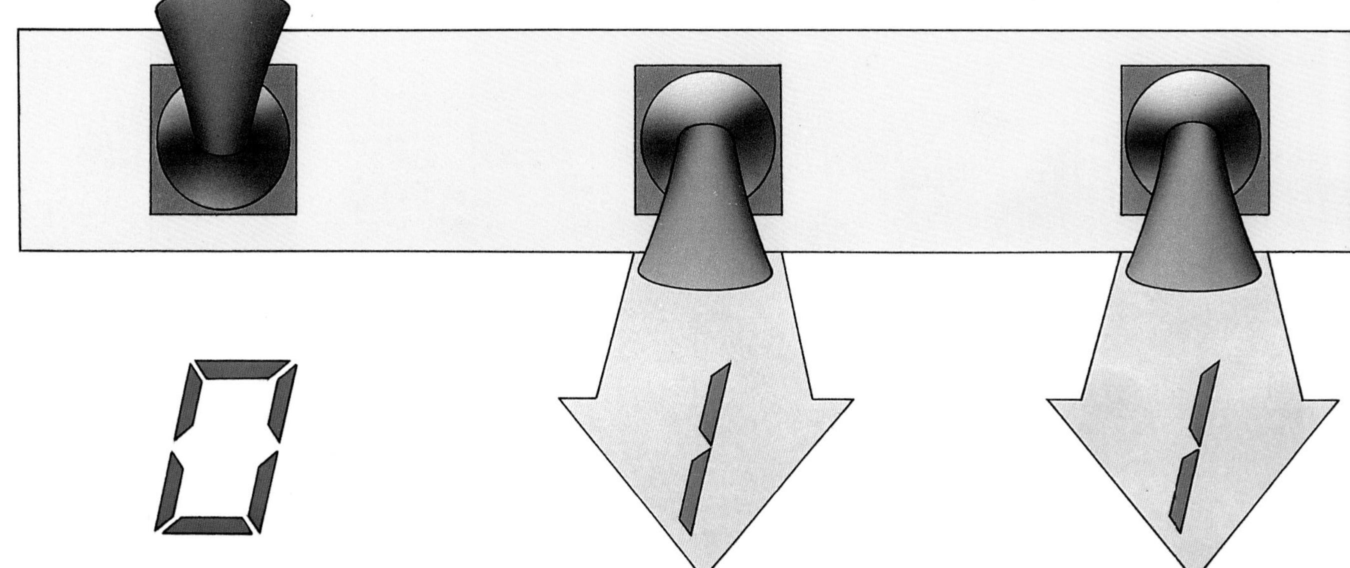

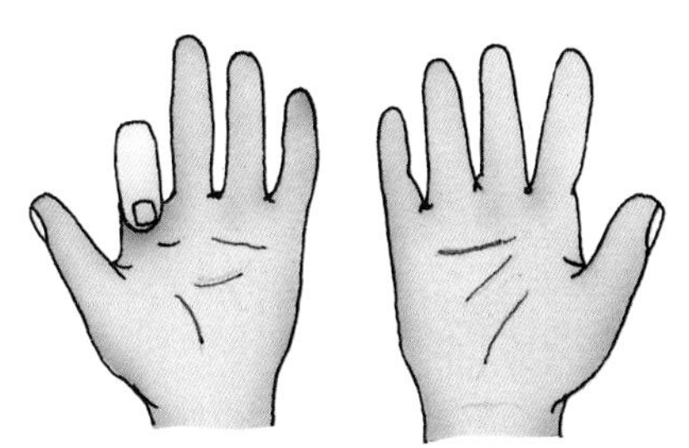

Do you know the trick that helps you with the multiplication table for 9? Hold up both hands, with palms facing you. If you want to work out 2 × 9, bend your second finger (counting your thumb). Now there is one finger to the left of the one you've bent, and eight to the right. So the answer is 18.

See if you can work out 5 × 9 by bending your fifth finger.

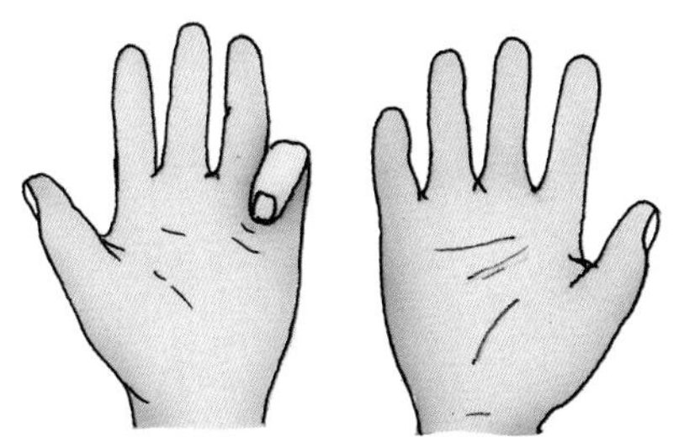

No skipping, please!

It might seem strange to make a flow chart about a simple thing like getting ready for school. You know perfectly well how to get to school without going to all that trouble.

But a computer cannot think for itself. It cannot say, "Oh, I've done that so many times that I don't need to think about it."

So if computers had to get ready for school, they would have to work through each step in the flow chart every time, but they could do this at amazing speed. The steps in the flow chart make up the **computer program.**

When you use a computer, you have to remember to work step by step. If you skip a step, the computer won't be able to find the right answer.

Using the binary system

Another important thing to remember about computers is that they work on base 2, or the binary system. It's helpful to think of a computer as a large number of electric switches. These switches can be only OFF (0) or ON (1). So the computer can work only in the binary numbers 0 and 1.

When you put base 10 numbers into the computer, it changes them into binary numbers before it works through the program. Then, when it has finished, it changes them back into base 10 numbers to give you the answer.

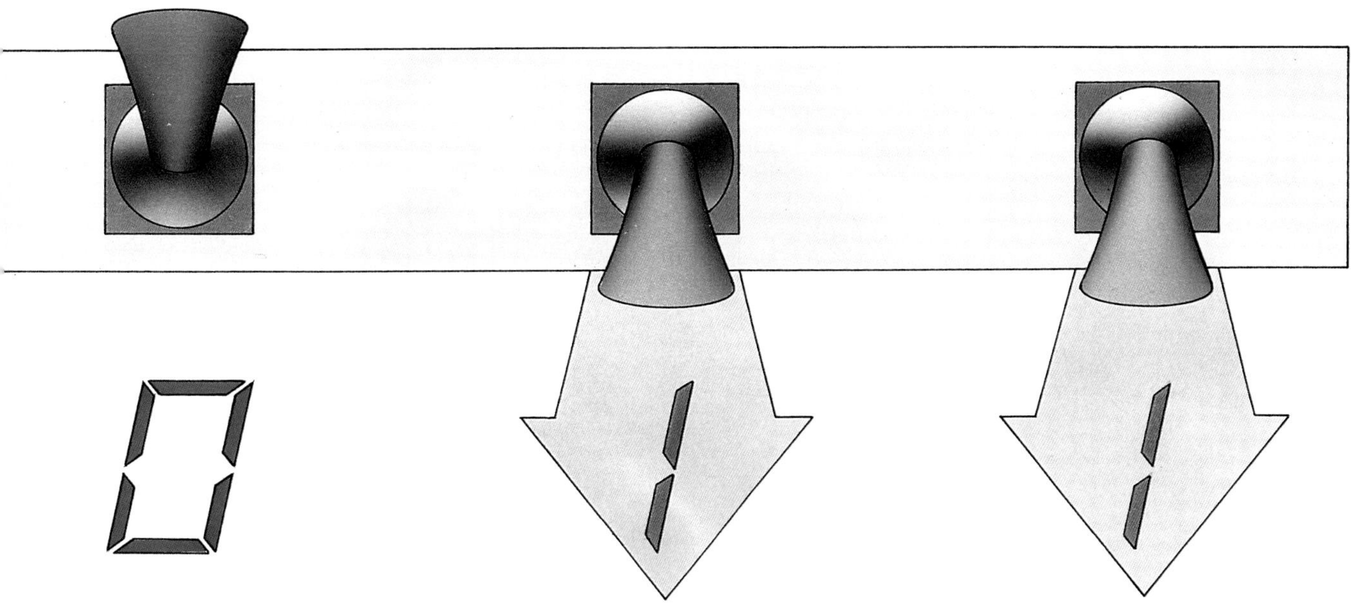

Find out more by looking at pages **14–15**

The pocket calculator

How quickly can you multiply 469 by 97? It will probably take you several minutes. But if you use a calculator, you'll get the answer in seconds.

When you use a **pocket,** or **hand, calculator,** you press the number keys on the keypad. The information you feed into the calculator is called the **input.** You use another key called a command key to tell the calculator what calculation you want it to perform. The answer that appears on the display panel is the **output.**

The power to make the calculator work usually comes from one or more batteries. Some calculators are powered by a cell which makes electrical energy from sunlight.

What can calculators do?

You can do all your adding, subtracting, multiplying, and dividing on the simplest calculator. Many calculators also have a key with a percentage sign on it and another with a square root symbol, so that you can work out percentages and square roots. The different things a calculator can do are called **functions.** Most calculators have a **memory** which stores numbers that you can use later.

The calculator will give out the correct answer because it never makes a mistake! But remember that calculators only work correctly if you key in the correct numbers and instructions. One of the reasons why calculators are so useful is that you can quickly check the answer to a calculation by doing it again.

Here is a number puzzle that you can solve with your calculator. It works in the same way as a crossword. Copy the grid onto a sheet of paper and fill in the answers. When you have completed this puzzle, try to make up some similar puzzles of your own.

Clues across

1. 4 × 18
3. 200 − 46
6. 9 × 87 + 120
8. 1150 ÷ 23
9. 2391 + 2691
11. 1976 − 176
14. How many 23's in 1587?
15. 819 − 493

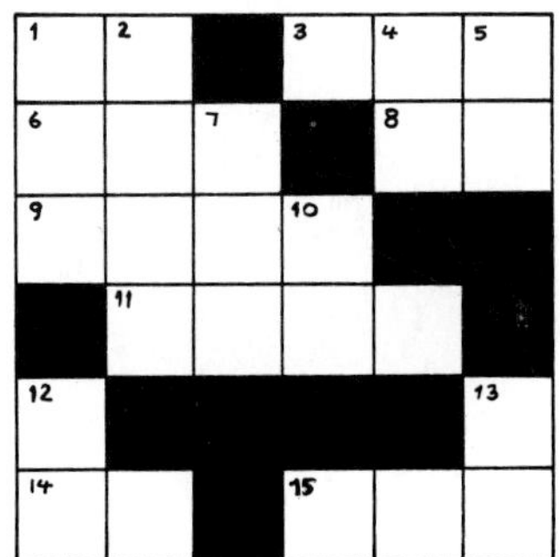

Clues down

1. 159 × 5
2. 957 + 1044
4. 68.75 ÷ 1.25
5. 300 ÷ 7.5
7. 516 − 128
10. 7300 ÷ 365
12. Which number × 18 makes 288?
13. How many years were there from 1876 to 1962?

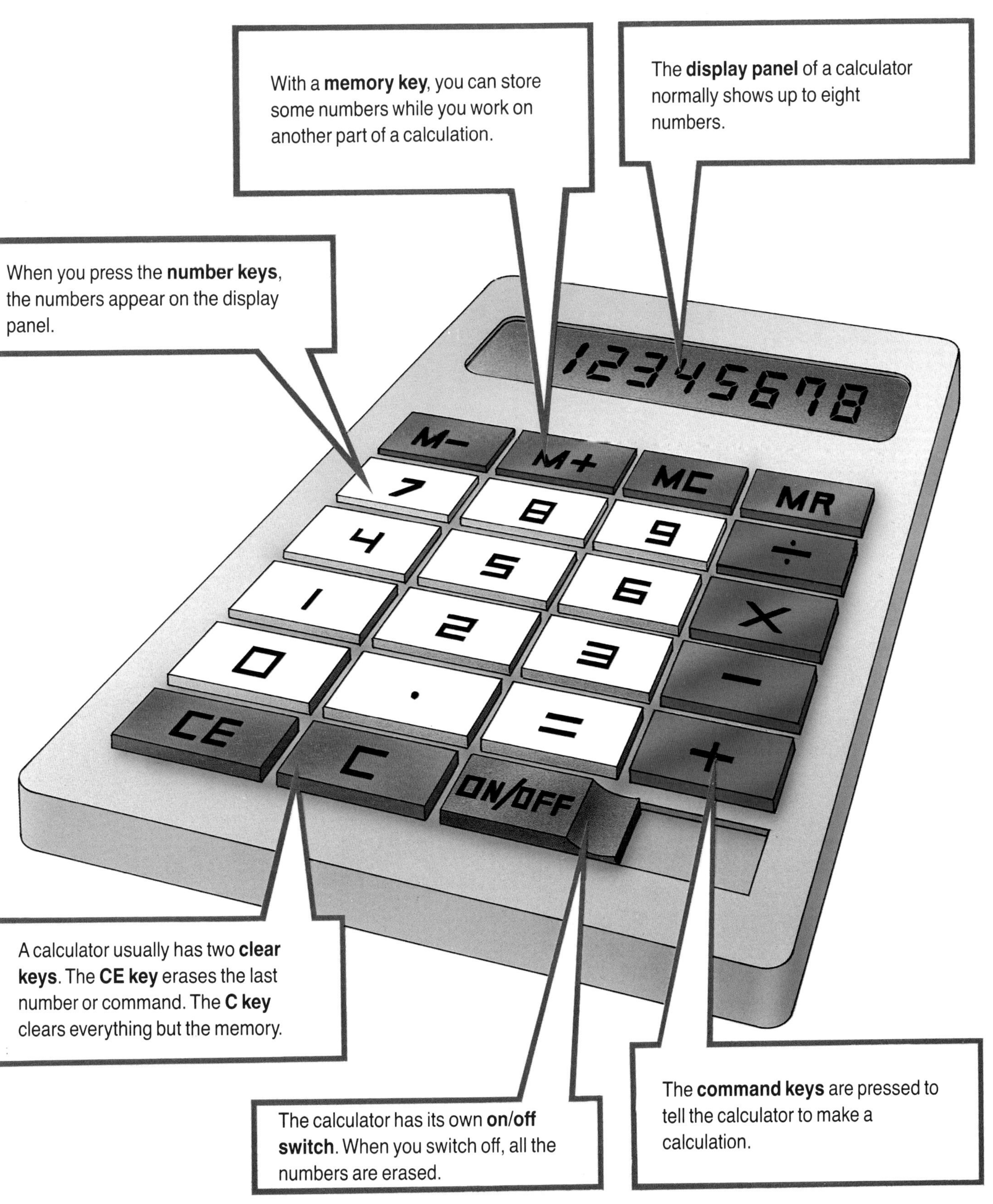
With a **memory key**, you can store some numbers while you work on another part of a calculation.
The **display panel** of a calculator normally shows up to eight numbers.
When you press the **number keys**, the numbers appear on the display panel.
12345678
M–
M+
MC
MR
7
8
9
÷
4
5
6
×
1
2
3
–
0
.
=
+
CE
C
ON/OFF
A calculator usually has two **clear keys**. The **CE key** erases the last number or command. The **C key** clears everything but the memory.
The calculator has its own **on/off switch**. When you switch off, all the numbers are erased.
The **command keys** are pressed to tell the calculator to make a calculation.

Analog or digital?

Do you have a watch? If so, does it have a face and two or three hands that move around? Or does it show the time in numbers? The first kind of watch is an **analog** instrument. The second is a **digital** instrument.

The word *analog,* also spelled *analogue,* means "similar" or "like." An analog instrument works like a copy of something that is happening in the real world. It imitates an activity and then shows what's happening on a scale, such as a dial.

You'll find an analog instrument in most cars in the form of a speedometer. How does it work? A cable runs from the speedometer to gears in the car's transmission. As the gears turn around, the cable turns a magnet. This spinning magnet pulls the needle across the dial to show the car's speed. The faster the wheels turn, the farther the needle moves. The turning of the car wheels is called the **stimulus,** and the movement of the needle on the speedometer dial is called the **response** to the stimulus.

A pantograph is an early analog instrument. It is used for producing larger or smaller copies, or models, of plans.

A model railway is an analog of the real thing. If it had enough track, it could be used to work out timetables for a real railway.

Analog and digital computers at work

Analog computers do not calculate using numbers. They imitate different parts of the problem and measure the results. **Digital computers** are the most common kind of computer today. They make calculations using numbers. Each calculation is carried out one step at a time. The answer is stored before the next step is begun. **Hybrid computers** imitate parts of the problem like an analog computer, but calculate using numbers like a digital computer.

Some of the instruments in front of the pilot of an aircraft are analog instruments. The fuel gauge shows how much fuel is left in the tank. The altimeter shows the height of the aircraft. How many other analog instruments can you see?

Find out more by looking at pages **32 – 33**
38 – 39

Computer words

If you want to understand computers and how they work, there are some important words you need to know.

Hardware and software

The different pieces of computer equipment are called **hardware.** A computer needs instructions to enable it to carry out a particular task. The series of instructions that the computer has to follow is called a **program.** The different programs that can be used in the computer are called **software.** Software is stored on hard, floppy, or compact disks. With different kinds of software, you can play games, do math problems, or type a letter. If you learn how to write programs, you can create your own software.

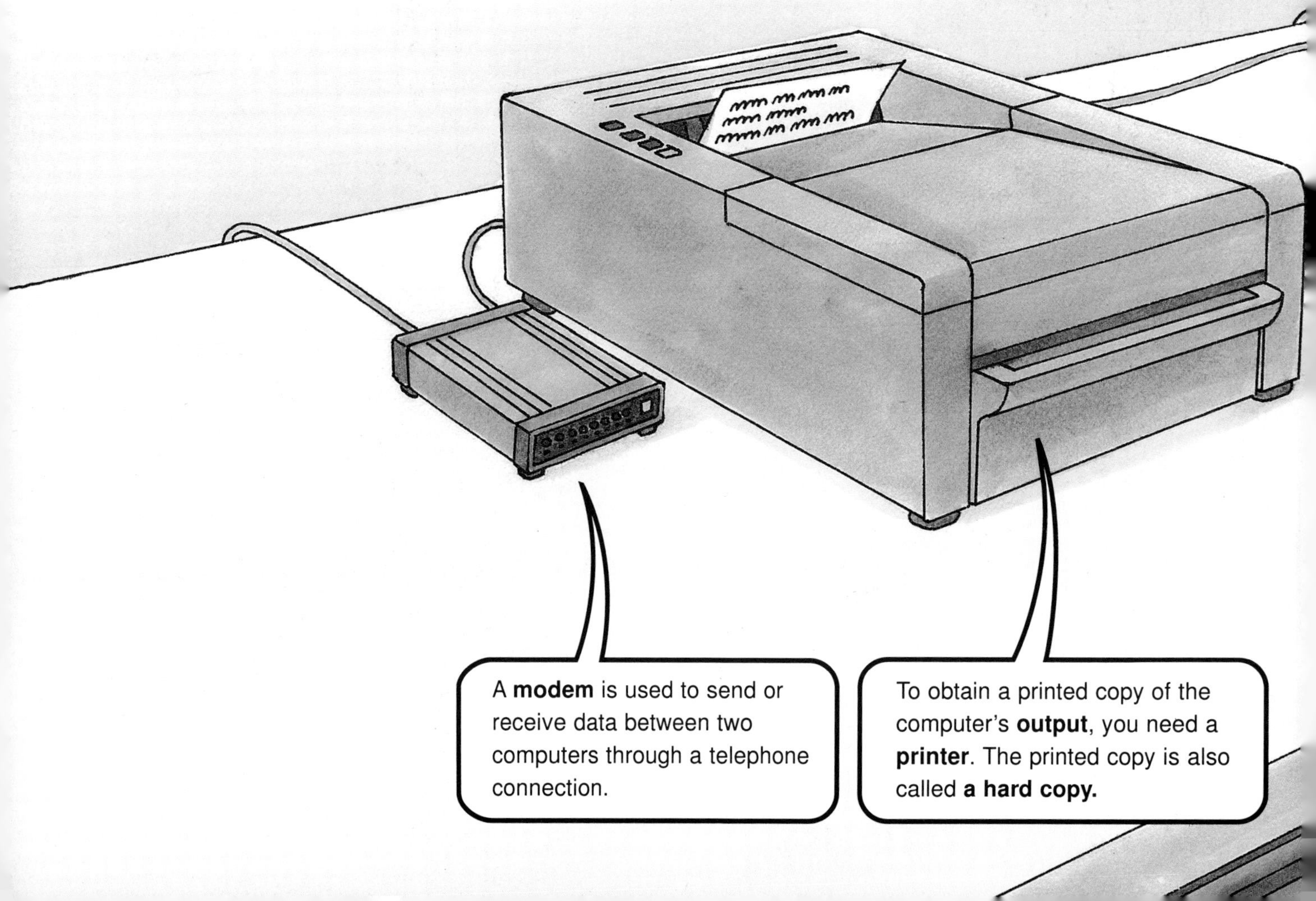

A **modem** is used to send or receive data between two computers through a telephone connection.

To obtain a printed copy of the computer's **output**, you need a **printer**. The printed copy is also called **a hard copy.**

The **monitor** has a screen like a television screen. It can display the computer's output and the information you type on the keyboard.

The **keyboard** is an **input device** because it feeds information into the computer. The information that is fed into the computer to enable it to carry out its task is called **data**.

A **mouse** is a small handheld device, usually connected by cable to the computer. By moving the mouse on the table, you control a pointer on the monitor screen. By clicking a button on the mouse, you can give the computer a command.

CD-ROMs are compact disks used to store information. A disk drive with a laser beam is used to read data from the CD. A standard CD-ROM cannot be changed or added to, unlike floppy or hard disks. CD-ROMs can contain several hundreds of times the information that a floppy disk can.

Flat pieces of magnetically coated plastic, called **floppy disks**, store information. The disks are protected in a plastic case.

Most personal computers have at least one floppy and one hard disk drive. Many also have a CD-ROM drive. **Disk drives** are needed to read and write information on a disk. A **hard disk drive** holds a permanently installed hard disk. **Hard disks** can store many times the amount of information that a floppy or compact disk can.

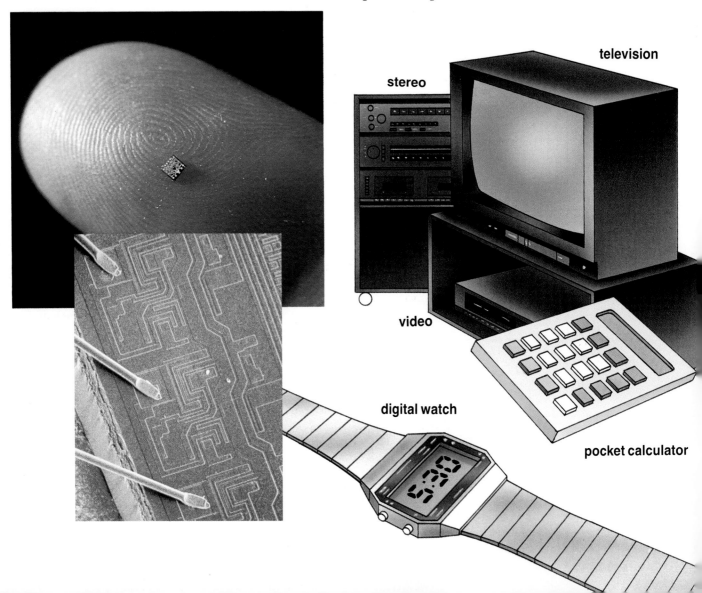

Find out more by looking at
pages **30 – 31**
36 – 37

Silicon chips

Computers no bigger than your fingertip? They exist, thanks to an amazing invention called the **integrated circuit,** also known as the **silicon chip** or just **chip.** Chips called **microprocessors,** which can perform all the functions of a computer, are so small that one will fit on the tip of your finger.

A chip is made from a very thin flake of a material called silicon. Specific areas of the chip are cut, or etched, in order to make a pattern called a **circuit.** This is a kind of pathway along which electric currents flow.

Chips today contain many millions of working parts, so small they can only be seen with a microscope. To keep the chip safe, the flake of silicon is sealed inside a ceramic, metal, or plastic case. Metal tags on the outside of the case are used to connect the chip to other parts and circuits.

This silicon chip, below, *is smaller than your fingertip. Take a closer look,* bottom picture, *and you can see that a chip contains circuits along which electric currents flow.*

television

stereo

video

digital watch

pocket calculator

Chips at home

How many chips are there in your home? You may be surprised at the answer. Chips control the household appliances in this picture. Chips switch on our alarm clock in the morning to wake us up. In a microwave oven, chips keep track of how long a meal has been cooking. In digital answering machines, messages are recorded directly onto a chip.

telephone and
digital answering machine

Chips inside your stereo and VCR

A chip inside the stereo cassette player can skip to the next song on a cassette tape by searching for the next blank spot on the tape. When you press the "play" button on the remote control device for the videocassette recorder (VCR), a chip tells the remote to send out a pulse of infrared light to the VCR. A chip inside the VCR receives and reads the signal, and signals the motor to roll the tape. The chips also allow you to program the VCR to record a television show that is scheduled to air several days later.

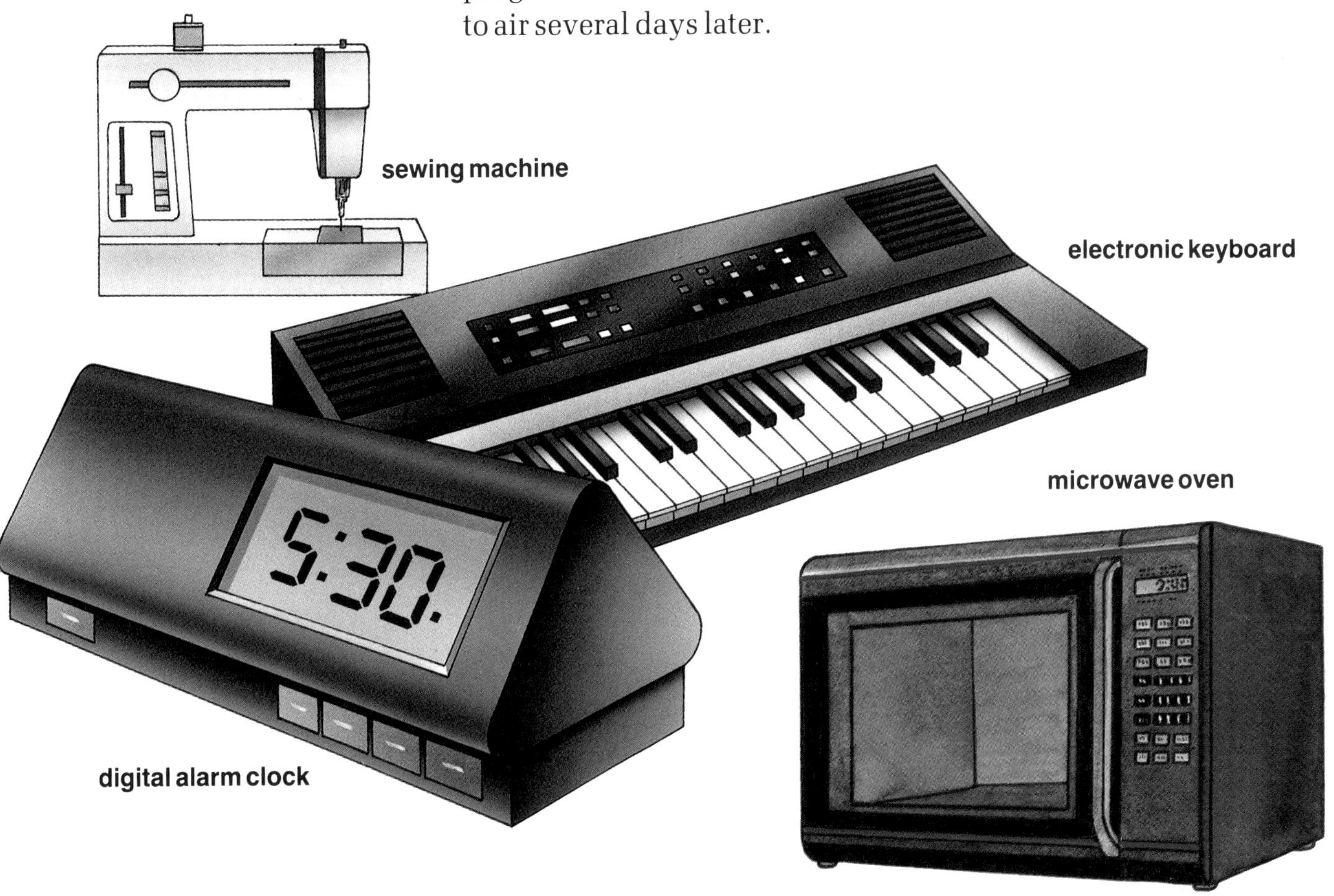

sewing machine

electronic keyboard

microwave oven

digital alarm clock

Find out more by looking at pages **12 – 13**
20 – 21

Bits, bytes, and gates

Here are more computer words you need to understand.

Bits and bytes

Remember that all computers use the binary system. There are two digits, 0 (NO) and 1 (YES). Each digit is called one **bit,** short for **b**inary dig**it.** In most microcomputers, a **byte** is eight bits. So a byte is any binary number between 00000000 and 11111111. Between these two numbers there are 256 different combinations of 0 and 1. Each combination or byte represents a numeral, a letter of the alphabet, a punctuation mark, or anything else that the computer can show. The more bytes a computer can store, the more work it can do. A computer's memory is measured in bytes. Many computers can hold hundreds of **megabytes** (1,048,576 bytes), and some can hold more than a **gigabyte** (1,000 megabytes) of information.

Bits flow along circuits in a computer rather like racing cars driving along a race track. The bits move along together in groups of eight, called bytes. Each byte represents a number, a letter, or a command.

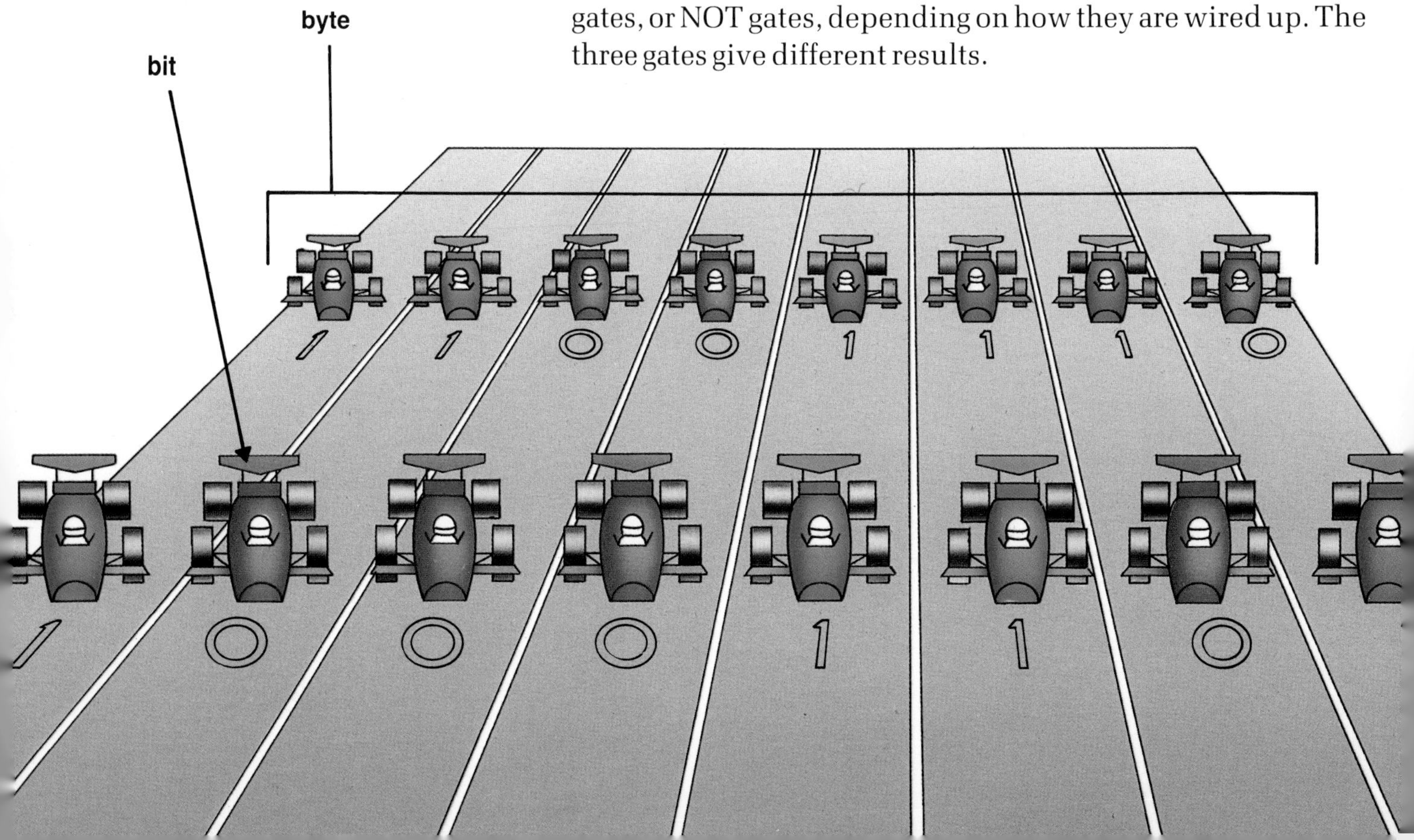

Gates

A computer carries out a task by breaking it down into small steps, like those of a flow chart. Each step is controlled by a group of electronic **gates.** These gates stop or let through one or both of two electric currents. Gates can be AND gates, OR gates, or NOT gates, depending on how they are wired up. The three gates give different results.

Through the gates

= current off.

= current flowing.

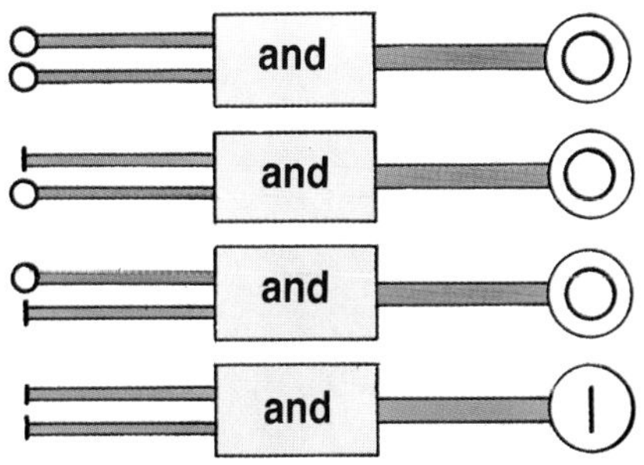

An AND gate will pass on an electric current only if there is current in both of the incoming wires.

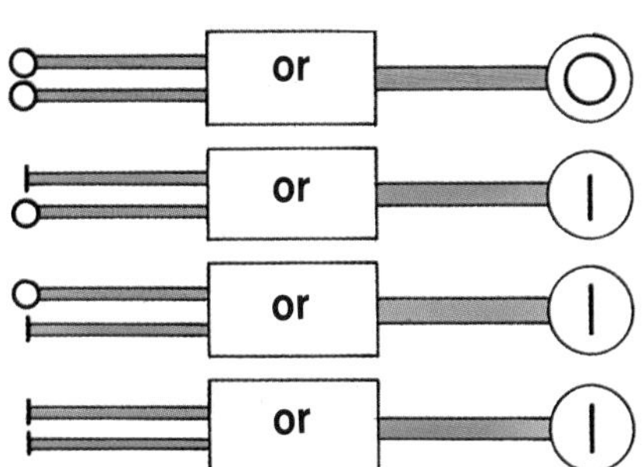

An OR gate will pass current on if either or both incoming wires have current in them.

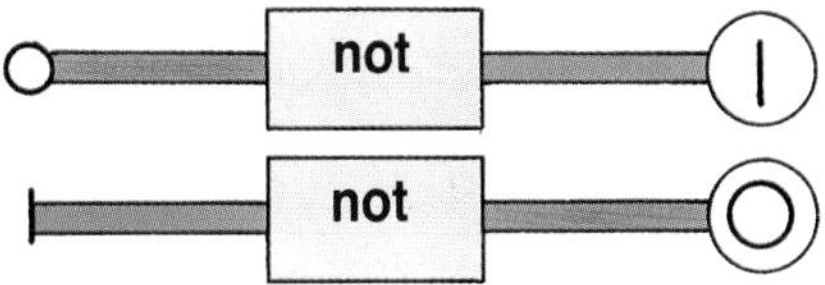

A NOT gate changes 1 into 0 or 0 into 1. It has one wire leading in and another leading out. A NOT gate changes, or inverts, the input it receives.

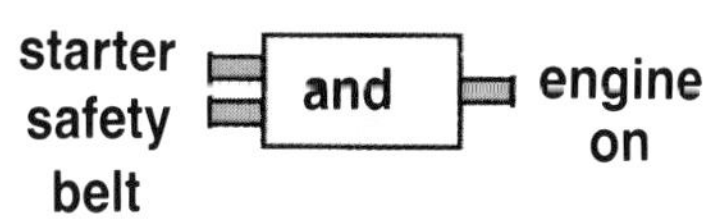

An AND gate in the wiring system of a car can prevent the car from starting until the driver fastens the safety belt. The gate will let current pass through to the starter motor only if there is current from the starter switch and from the safety belt catch.

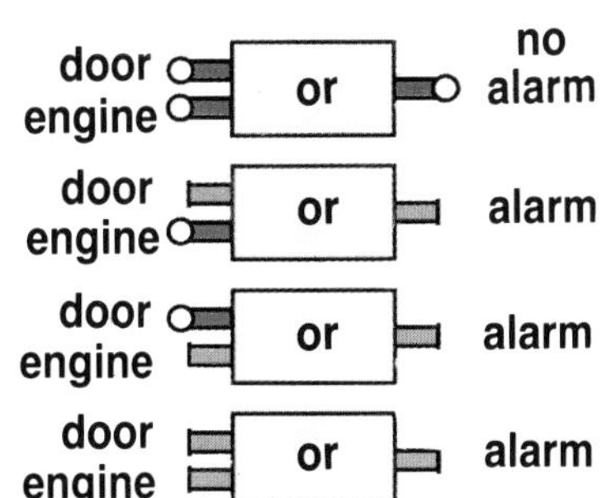

A car alarm system uses an OR gate. If the door is closed and the engine is switched off, no current passes through. But if a thief forces the door open or starts the engine, or both, current passes through the gate and an alarm sounds.

Find out more by looking at pages **30–31**
32–33

Types of computers

How big do you think a computer is? Computers come in many different sizes. A computer can be big enough to fill a room about the size of a school hall, or small enough to rest in the palm of your hand.

The largest computers are called **mainframe** computers. Unlike personal computers, mainframes are designed to be used by many people at once. Each person works from a **terminal,** which has a monitor, a keyboard, and sometimes other hardware. Mainframes are often found in the head offices of large companies. **Supercomputers** are the fastest and most powerful mainframe computers. They are used to calculate very complex mathematical problems, such as predicting the path and behavior of a tornado.

Because they give off so much heat, mainframe computers are housed in special air-conditioned, dust-free rooms.

From mainframe to palmtop

Over the years, computers have grown smaller, faster, and easier to use. Early mainframe computers filled entire rooms and needed a team of people to operate them. In the early 1960's, the development of the **integrated circuit** on a silicon chip enabled **minicomputers**— about the size of a china cabinet—to be built.

The next step forward came in 1971 when the first **microprocessors** were produced. A microprocessor combines all of a computer's basic functions on a single chip. Microprocessors are at the heart of **microcomputers,** also called personal computers (PC's), which first appeared in the mid-1970's. The first PC's were small enough to fit on a desk.

Computers kept getting smaller. The first **portable computer,** which was the size of a small suitcase, was introduced in 1983. Today, many business people carry **laptop** or **notebook computers,** which are small enough to sit comfortably on your lap. **Handheld** personal computers, including **palmtop computers** and **personal digital assistants** (PDA's), are light and small enough to be held in your hand. To use some PDA's, you write with a pencillike stylus directly on the screen.

laptop computer

palmtop computer

Computer systems

We often talk about computers when we really mean **computer systems.** The computer is only one part of the system. It cannot work on its own. It needs an input, with which we can feed in data and programs, and an output, which gives us the results of the computer's task. The many parts of the computer equipment are called hardware. The computer's heart is the **central processing unit** (CPU). This contains many parts. The two most important are the **control unit** (CU) and the **arithmetic/logic unit** (ALU).

The CU collects information from the input and the memory. It then passes instructions to the ALU and stores the information after it has been used. If you use a keyboard as an input, everything you tap on the keys must be changed into binary code. Similarly, when the computer has finished its task, the results in binary code must be changed back into decimal numbers, words or pictures that appear on the monitor.

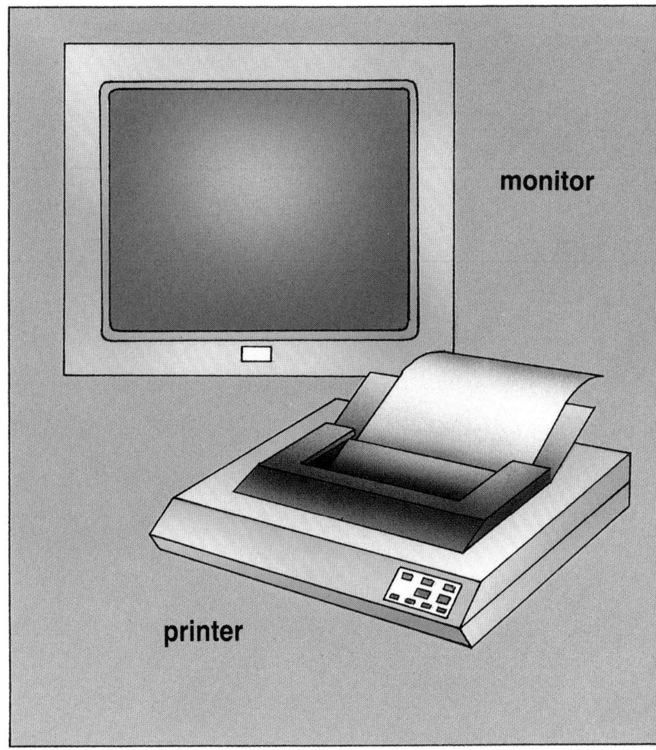

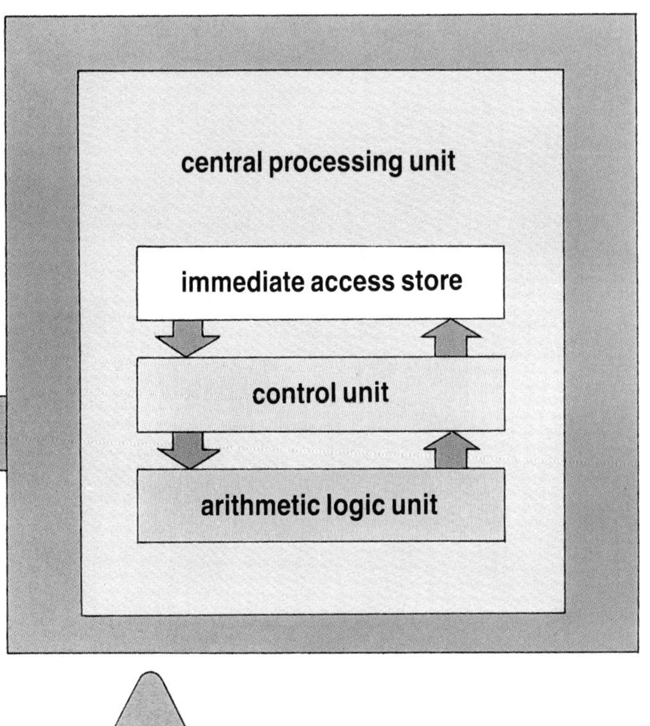

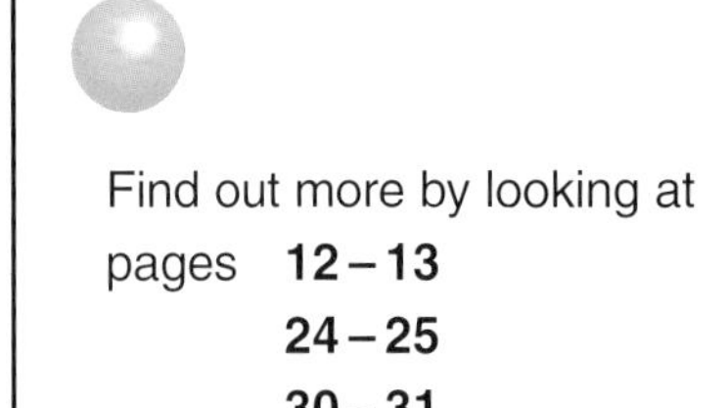
Find out more by looking at
pages 12 – 13
24 – 25
30 – 31

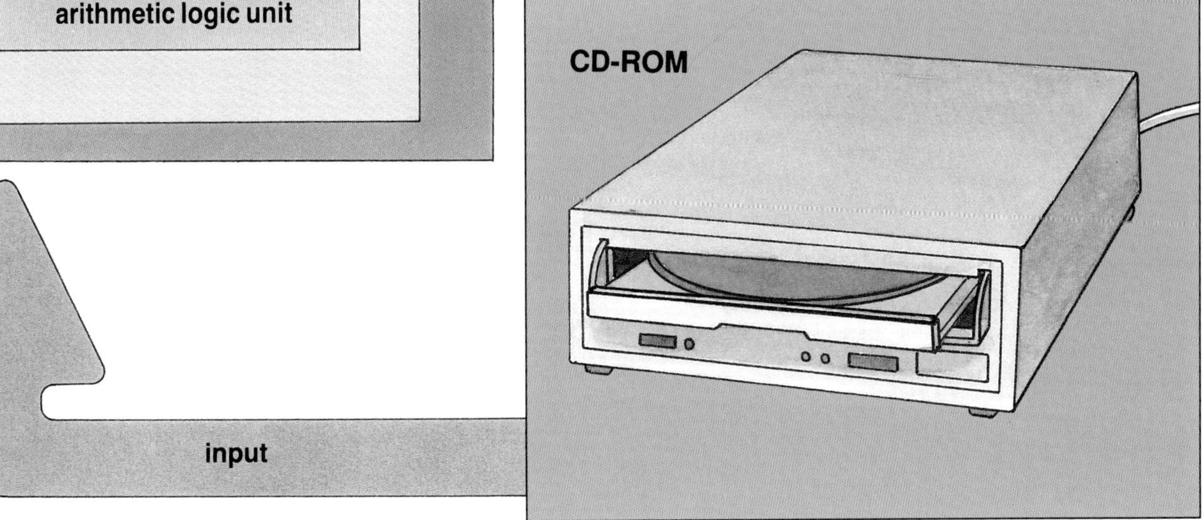

Computer systems have an input, a CPU, and an output.

The ALU does all the calculations needed for the task. It contains a series of gates of different types. The **immediate access store** (IAS) stores programs and data while the task is being done. The IAS is one part of the computer's memory.

Keeping in step

When a computer is working through a program, information passes backward and forward at high speed. To keep all the movements in step, there is a clock that starts to beat time as soon as the computer is switched on. Have you ever watched an orchestra playing? If so, you will have seen how the conductor keeps time with a baton. The clock in a computer does a similar job with all the electric currents that move about as the computer carries out its task.

Controlling a computer

Some people think that what goes on inside a computer is magic. The truth is that there is no magic at all. A computer is simply a machine.

To make a car work the way you want it to, you have to operate the controls in a certain way. It is just the same with a computer. Cars and computers will only do what you make them do.

The input is the part of a computer system that tells the computer what to do and gives the computer the information it needs to perform the task. The keyboard, modem, mouse, disk, and disk drive can all be used to input information. Here are some of the many other types of input devices.

*A **voice recognition system** lets a computer understand and respond to human speech. A computer with voice recognition software will respond to commands spoken into a microphone (such as "insert disk" and "open file"), or it will "type" your words onto the screen. These systems are very useful for disabled persons who can speak but cannot move computer hardware or type.*

***Joysticks** are often used to play computer games, but they are also sometimes used to create technical drawings, such as the plans for a house.*

*A **scanner** "reads" images on a page and translates them into digital signals the computer can understand. The image data can be stored in a file and displayed on the monitor. Optical character recognition (OCR) software recognizes the shapes of letters and characters. Using a scanner and OCR software, you can input a printed document without typing.*

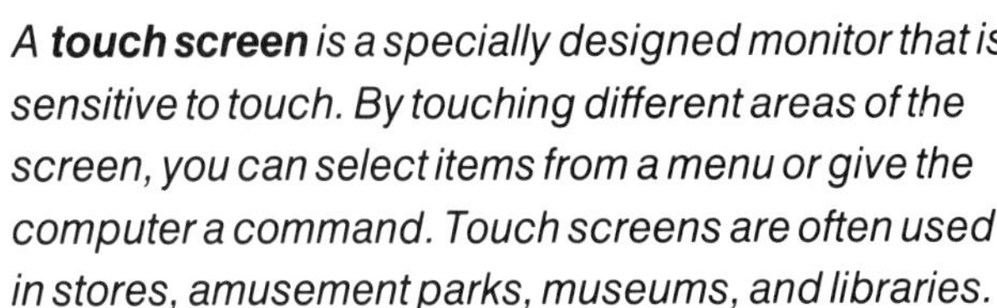

*A **touch screen** is a specially designed monitor that is sensitive to touch. By touching different areas of the screen, you can select items from a menu or give the computer a command. Touch screens are often used in stores, amusement parks, museums, and libraries.*

*A **trackball** is similar to a mouse. You roll a small ball with your fingers to move a pointer on the screen. The trackball is sometimes part of the keyboard, especially on laptop computers. It can also be separate from the keyboard. A trackball device has buttons like a mouse, which are used to give the computer commands.*

*A **graphic tablet** has a special pad and pen for drawing pictures. The pictures can be seen on the screen and can be stored in the computer's memory.*

Memory

Imagine that you are going to the park to play with your friends. You know the way because you have been there before. The route is stored in your memory. On the way, you meet someone and stop for a chat. If your chat is not about anything important, you will probably soon forget it. Your memory does not store everything forever.

The disk drive reads a program and data from a disk and feeds it into the RAM.

How a computer remembers

A computer's memory works in a similar way. There are some pieces of information that need to be stored away. Others can be forgotten once the computer has worked on them. To separate the two types of information, a computer has two memories, called **ROM** and **RAM.**

ROM stands for **read-only memory.** ROM carries the information the computer needs to carry out its tasks. This information is built into the computer and cannot be altered. It stays there even when the computer is switched off, just as your memory of how to get to the park stays with you until you need it again.

RAM stands for **random access memory,** or read and write memory. This contains the information the computer needs to carry out the particular task you want it to do now. When you switch off the computer, RAM empties itself. You can save your work on disk. Next time you use the computer, you will have to feed in the program again, together with new data and commands.

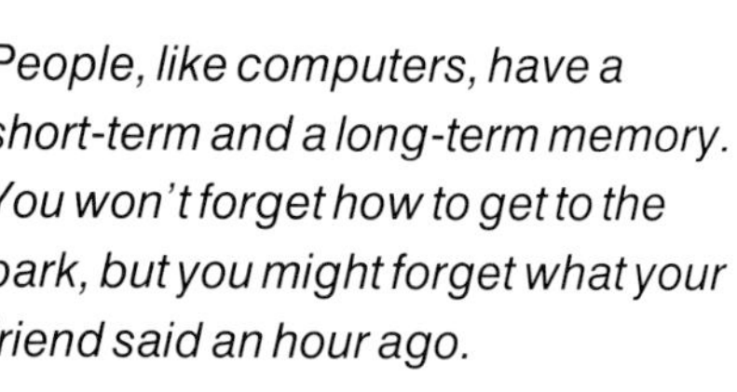

People, like computers, have a short-term and a long-term memory. You won't forget how to get to the park, but you might forget what your friend said an hour ago.

Find out more by looking at
pages **32–33**
36–37
38–39

Storing information

ROM and RAM are both made up of **memory cells.** Each memory cell stores binary digits. A chip may be able to store many thousands of bits. It is easy to see that the size of a computer's RAM is important, because the computer can only do the amount of work that its RAM has room for. With some computers, it is possible to add extra **memory chips** to increase the RAM.

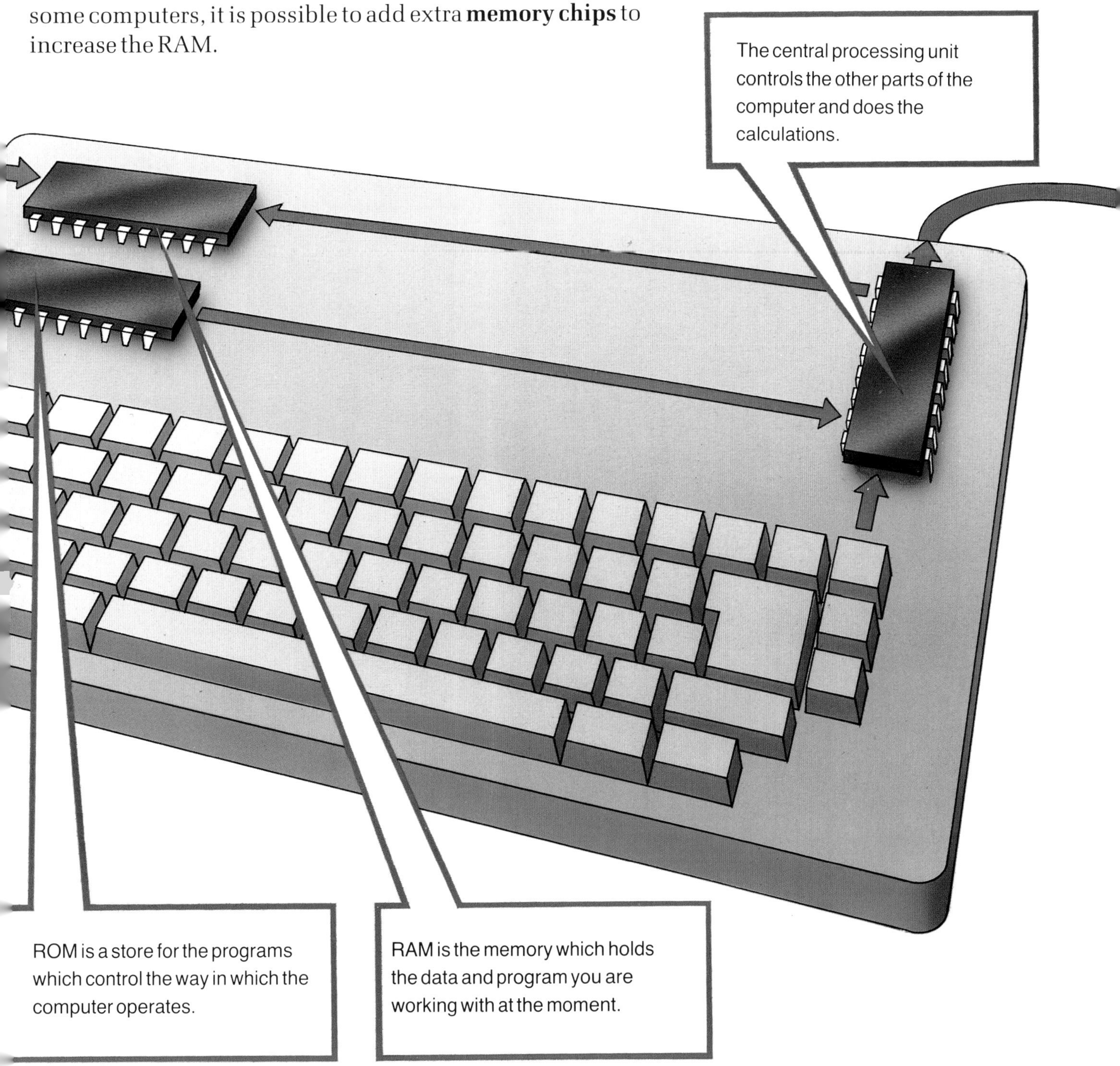

The central processing unit controls the other parts of the computer and does the calculations.

ROM is a store for the programs which control the way in which the computer operates.

RAM is the memory which holds the data and program you are working with at the moment.

Find out more by looking at pages **30 – 31**
46 – 47

Computer software

The list of different things you can do with the help of a computer is almost endless. You can play chess with a computer, write a story or a letter, keep a diary, keep a record of the addresses of your friends, or draw a three-dimensional robot. With a CD-ROM player, you can take a tour of the human body, featuring an animated "flight" down the center of a spine. Or you can look up a recent president in a CD-ROM encyclopedia, look at his picture, read about him, and then hear him speak. In business, computers are often used to predict future business activity—for instance, to estimate how many computers people will buy next year!

Different types of computer software let you play games and do other tasks using your computer.

Programs and other information are stored on CD-ROMs and floppy disks.

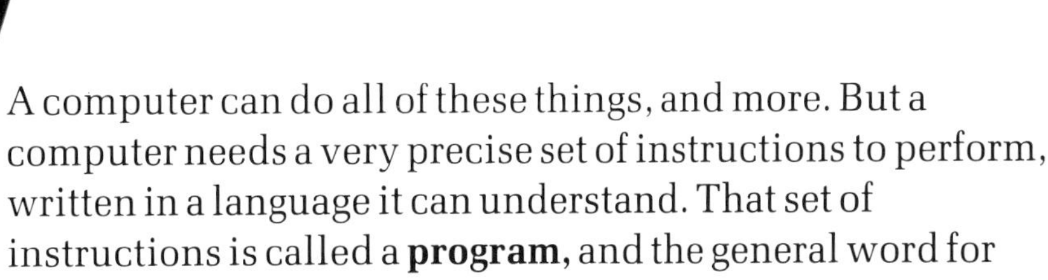

A computer can do all of these things, and more. But a computer needs a very precise set of instructions to perform, written in a language it can understand. That set of instructions is called a **program,** and the general word for computer programs is **software.**

Software can be purchased at a store or by mail through a catalog. The software package usually includes a manual with instructions on how to use the program and how to copy the program onto your computer's hard disk drive. The program itself comes on a floppy disk or disks, or sometimes on a CD-ROM. CD-ROMs may include text, pictures, sound, and even moving pictures. Programs that combine several of these formats, or media, are called **multimedia** programs.

A **virus** is a kind of program that you *don't* want on your computer. Often hidden or disguised, a virus tampers with or damages programs and data on your computer. Virus detection programs check for and destroy any viruses, and attempt to repair any damage.

Because floppy disks and even hard disks can become damaged or unusable, it is always important to make backup copies of your software onto blank floppy disks. Keep your floppy disks—and your computer—away from magnets. A magnet can quickly erase all of the software on a disk!

Programs and programming languages

Software programs are written by **programmers** (people who write programs) in a special **programming language** that computers can interpret and understand. Every programming language has a strict set of rules, called **syntax,** that must be followed. If one word or letter is out of place, the program may shut down. This kind of mistake is called a **bug,** and a big part of writing a program is fixing bugs.

Many different programming languages have been invented, such as COBOL, Pascal, Fortran, and LISP. The language called C is popular among professional programmers. Simple languages called BASIC and Logo are easy to learn and good for students and beginners.

Solving a problem

Before you write a program, you have to decide what problem you want the computer to solve. Then you have to break the problem down into steps. One way of doing this is to make a flow chart.

Here is a problem. Galileo Galilei was a famous scientist who was born in 1564. In 1609, he made his first telescope. How old was he then?

The task is to subtract 1564 from 1609. A flow chart of the problem looks like this.

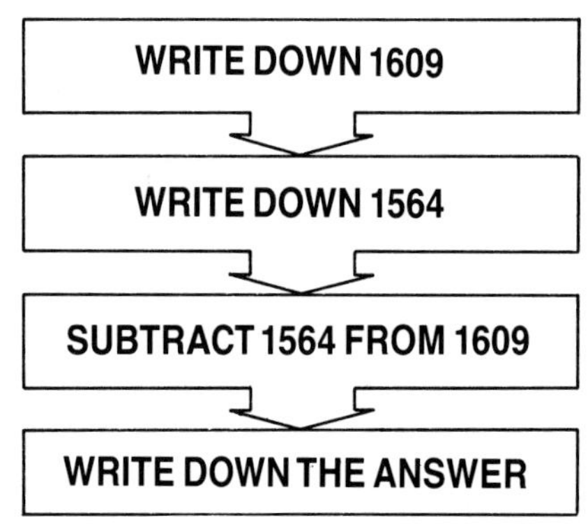

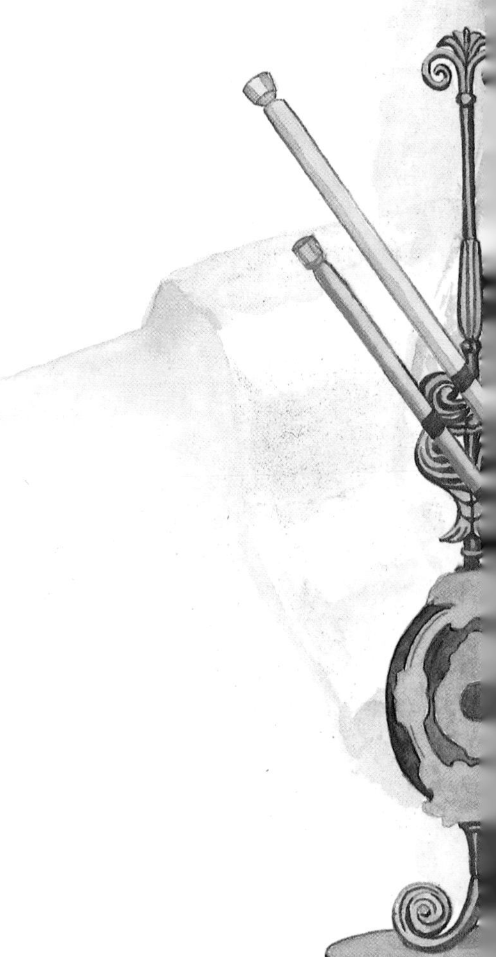

Writing in BASIC

On the screen, you can see how this flow chart is written as a program in BASIC. The first line has the title of the program. The words in the other lines are instructions that the computer understands. They help tell the computer how to do the task you want it to do. If you have a personal computer that understands BASIC, try the program for yourself. You may need to work at school.

```
REMARK    Age of Galileo

PRINT    "Galileo was born in 1564."
LET    BornDate = 1564

PRINT    "Enter Telescope date"
INPUT    TelDate

LET    Age = TelDate – BornDate
PRINT    "Galileo was then"; Age

END
RUN
```

Find out more by looking at pages **30 – 31**

Writing by computer

Have you ever used a typewriter? If you leave something out, you may have to type the whole piece of work again. If you want to change some words or the margins, you also will probably have to type the entire document again.

With **word-processing software,** you can use your computer to create a document, such as a letter or story, change it, print it, and save it for further use. You can change parts of the document without having to retype all of it. When you use a word-processing program, your typing appears on the screen. The program lets you make corrections, insert new words and sentences, and copy or move a portion of text from one place in the document to another. It will even check your spelling!

If you want to stop work and carry on later, you can save, or file, your document on your computer's hard disk or on a floppy disk. Finally, when your work is ready, you print it out using a printer.

If you look closely at a letter printed on a dot matrix printer, you'll see that it is made up of tiny dots.

Printing by dots, jets, and lasers

A **dot matrix printer** produces a pattern, or matrix, of dots in the shape of a letter. Small metal pins push against an ink ribbon, transferring the pattern to paper. An **ink jet printer** creates letter patterns by shooting heated liquid ink onto the page through very small jet nozzles.

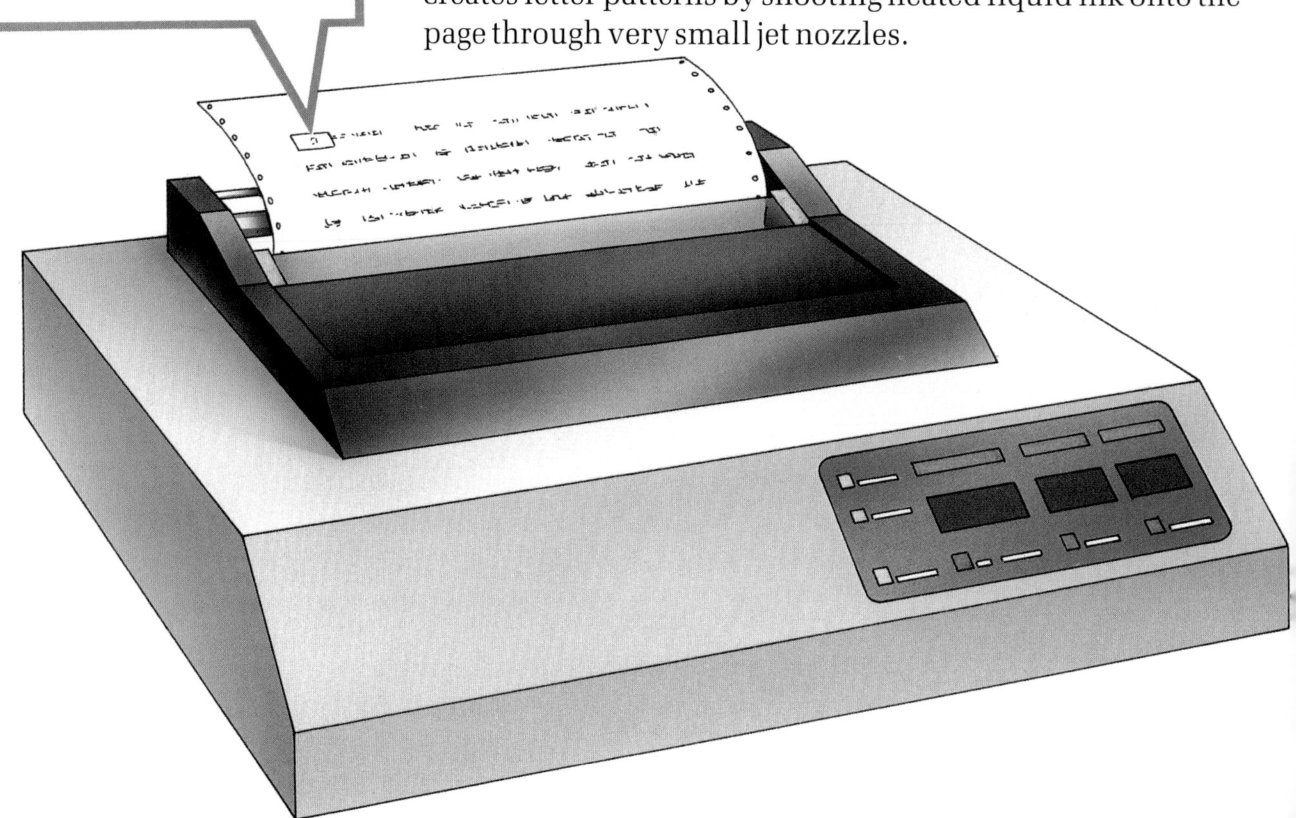

Laser printers are the fastest printers available for personal computers. A laser printer uses a beam of laser light to create an electrically charged image on a rotating cylinder. The charged areas attract **toner** (powdered or liquid ink). The cylinder transfers the toner, and thus the image, onto paper as the two come into contact. The paper then passes through fuser rollers, which cause the toner to fuse to the page.

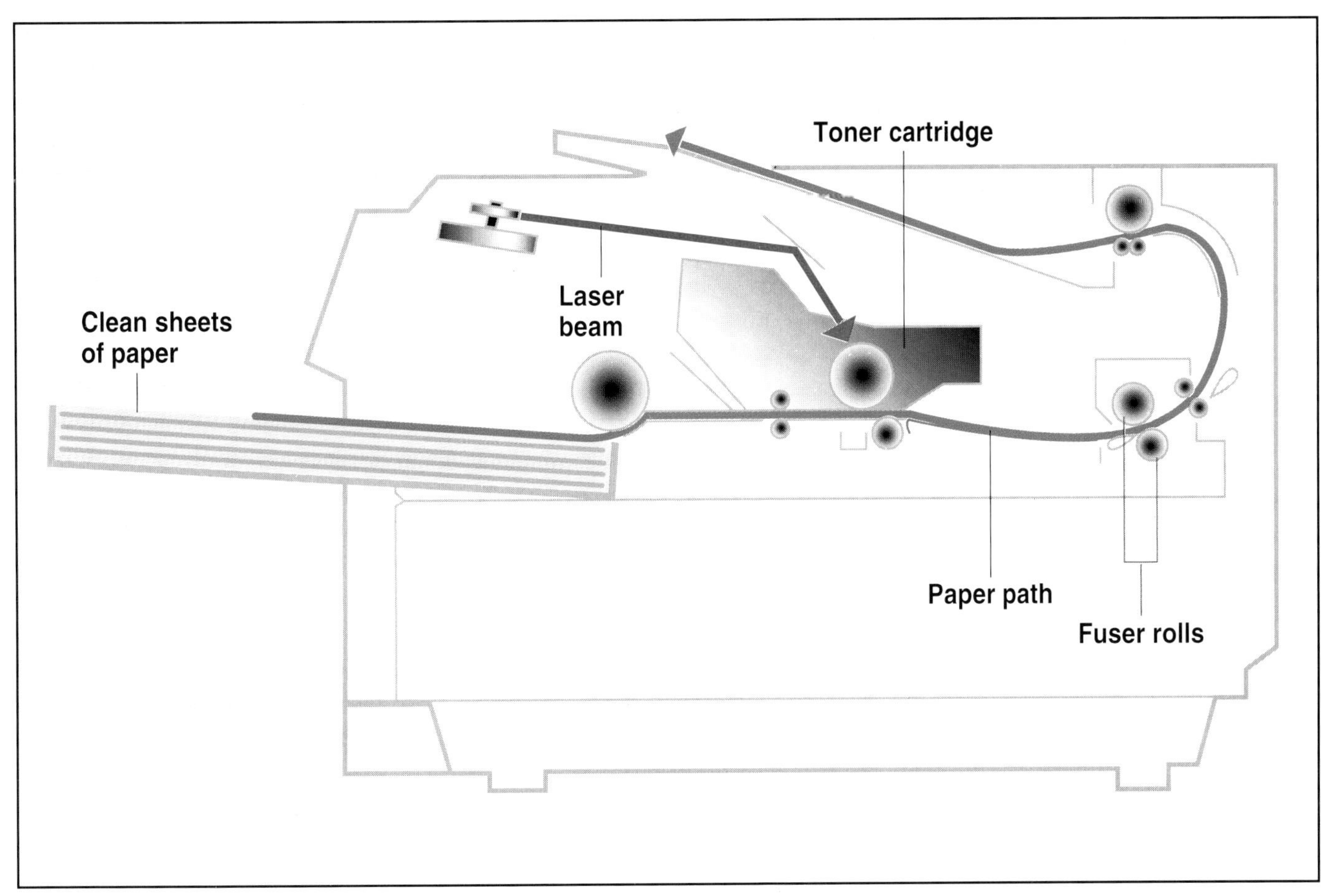

Find out more by looking at
pages **32–33**
40–41

Computers in daily life

Ali and his mother want to go shopping, but there is no money in the house and the banks are closed. How will they manage? They go to a special machine, an **ATM** (Automatic Teller Machine). These machines are located outside banks, in shopping malls, and at various other locations. Ali's mother puts her bank card into a slot and types her code number on the keyboard. She keys in the amount of money they need and the bills come out.

The machine is linked to a computer that checks the name of Ali's mother and her code number, makes sure there is enough money in her account, and then signals the machine to pay out the amount requested.

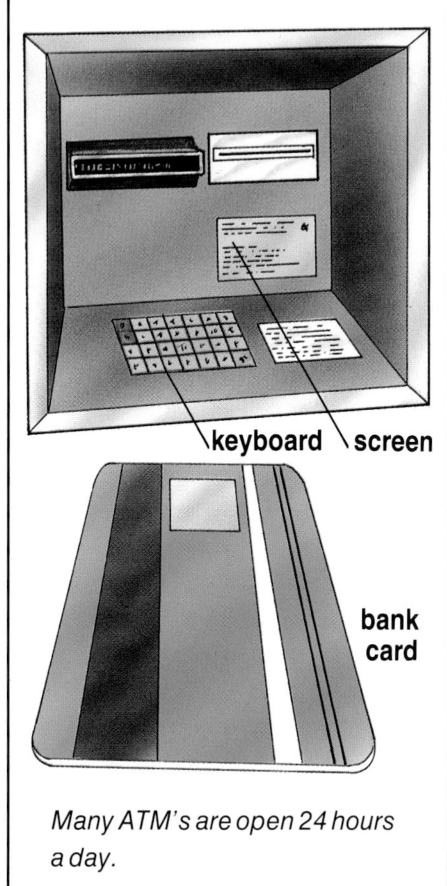

Many ATM's are open 24 hours a day.

What is a bar code?

At the supermarket, Ali wants to buy cookies. In a rectangle on the packet is a set of lines called a **bar code.** The cashier can pass a laser pen over the bar code or pass the item over a laser scanner. The price then appears on a screen.

Bar codes on consumer goods give information to a computer.

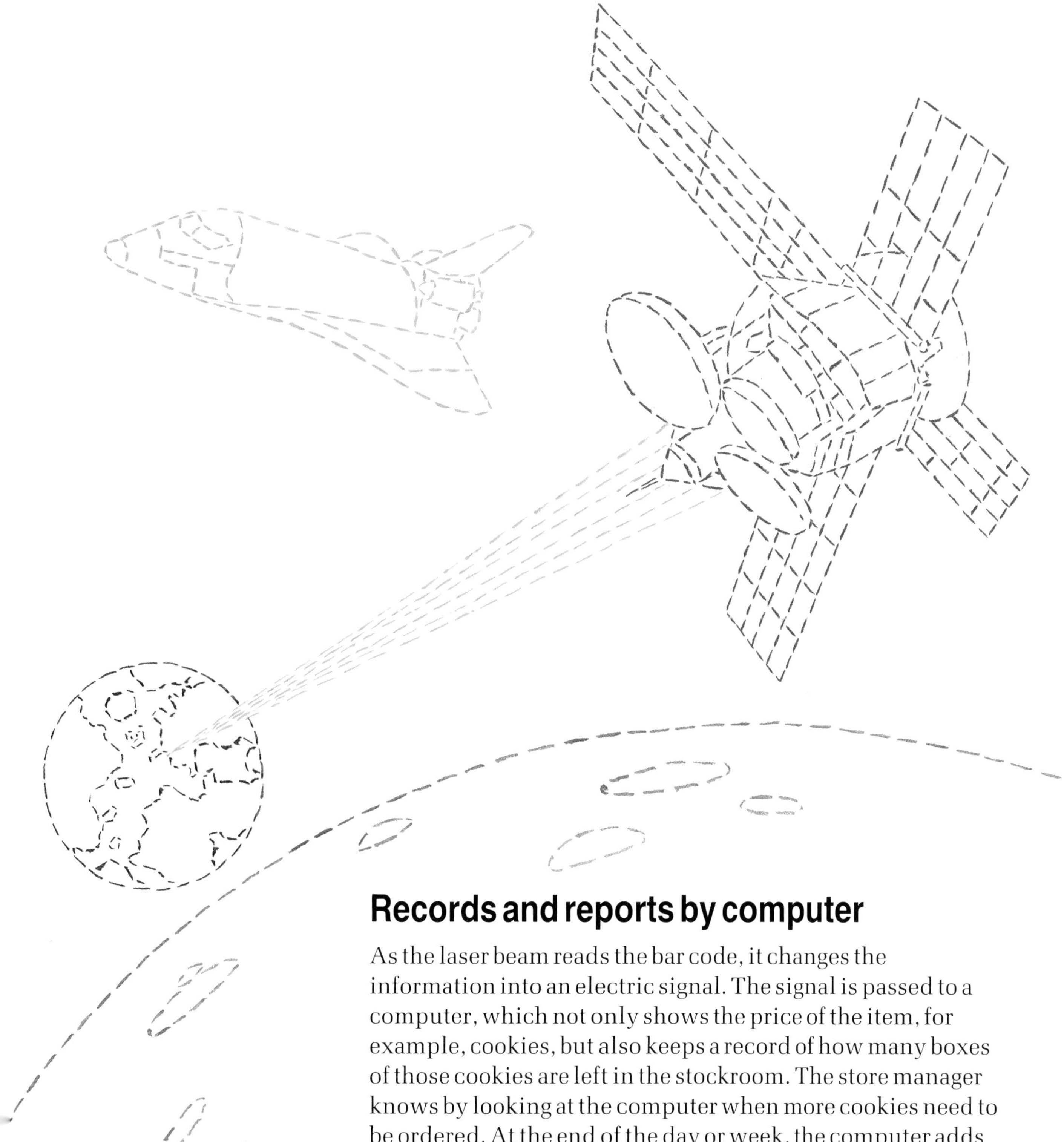

Records and reports by computer

As the laser beam reads the bar code, it changes the information into an electric signal. The signal is passed to a computer, which not only shows the price of the item, for example, cookies, but also keeps a record of how many boxes of those cookies are left in the stockroom. The store manager knows by looking at the computer when more cookies need to be ordered. At the end of the day or week, the computer adds up how many of each item have been sold. The manager can then send an order to the warehouse for fresh supplies.

There is a newspaper stand outside the supermarket. Ali stops to buy a paper. On the front page is a report about a spacecraft on its way to the planet Venus. Ali may not realize it, but this report would not be possible without computers. Computers have collected data from the spacecraft. A reporter has used a word processor and a modem to send the story along a telephone line to an editor at the newspaper office.

What is a database?

Say that you want to find a book on computers at your local library. In some libraries, the library catalog, or list of resources available, is still on typed index cards, which are stored in file drawers. Looking up "computer" in the "c" file drawer is quicker than searching through the shelves, but it can still take you a long time to find what you are looking for.

Because of their fast speeds and large memories, computers are very good at storing large amounts of information. Information stored in a **database** is organized in a way that makes the information easy to retrieve. In most libraries today, the catalog of books is stored in a computer database, rather than on index cards. The computer lets you find the book you are looking for in much less time. Sometimes it can even tell you if the book is available at another library.

Searching databases for information

Information is put into a database by categories; the place in the database for each category is called a **field.** Each entry in the database is called a **record.** Records in a library catalog database, for instance, will include fields for title, author, subject, publisher, and copyright date. To find all the books written *by* Joe Smith, the computer looks at the "author" field in each entry to see if it contains the words "Joe Smith." But to find all the books *about* Joe Smith, the computer looks at the "subject" field. When it has finished searching, the computer displays on the monitor all the entries it has found. Then you can print them out.

Databases can store enormous amounts of information. For example, they are used by hospitals to keep records of patients; by governments to store census and election information; and by businesses who offer on-line (over the telephone) access to computer databases such as encyclopedias, right.

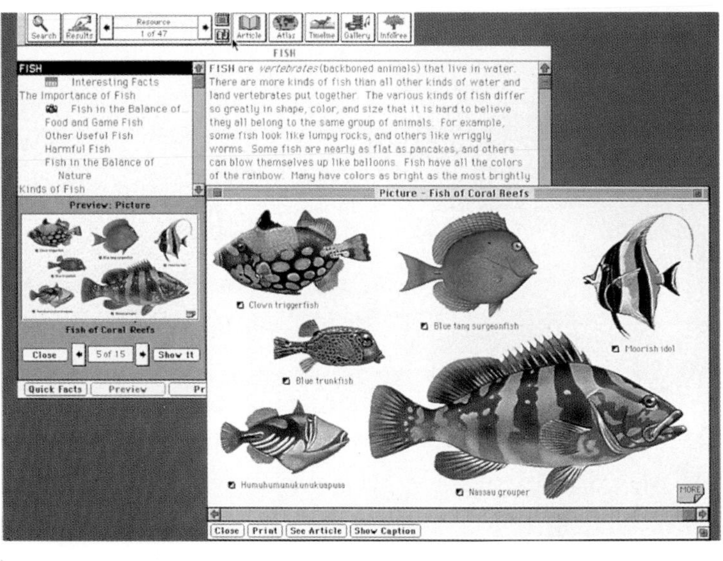

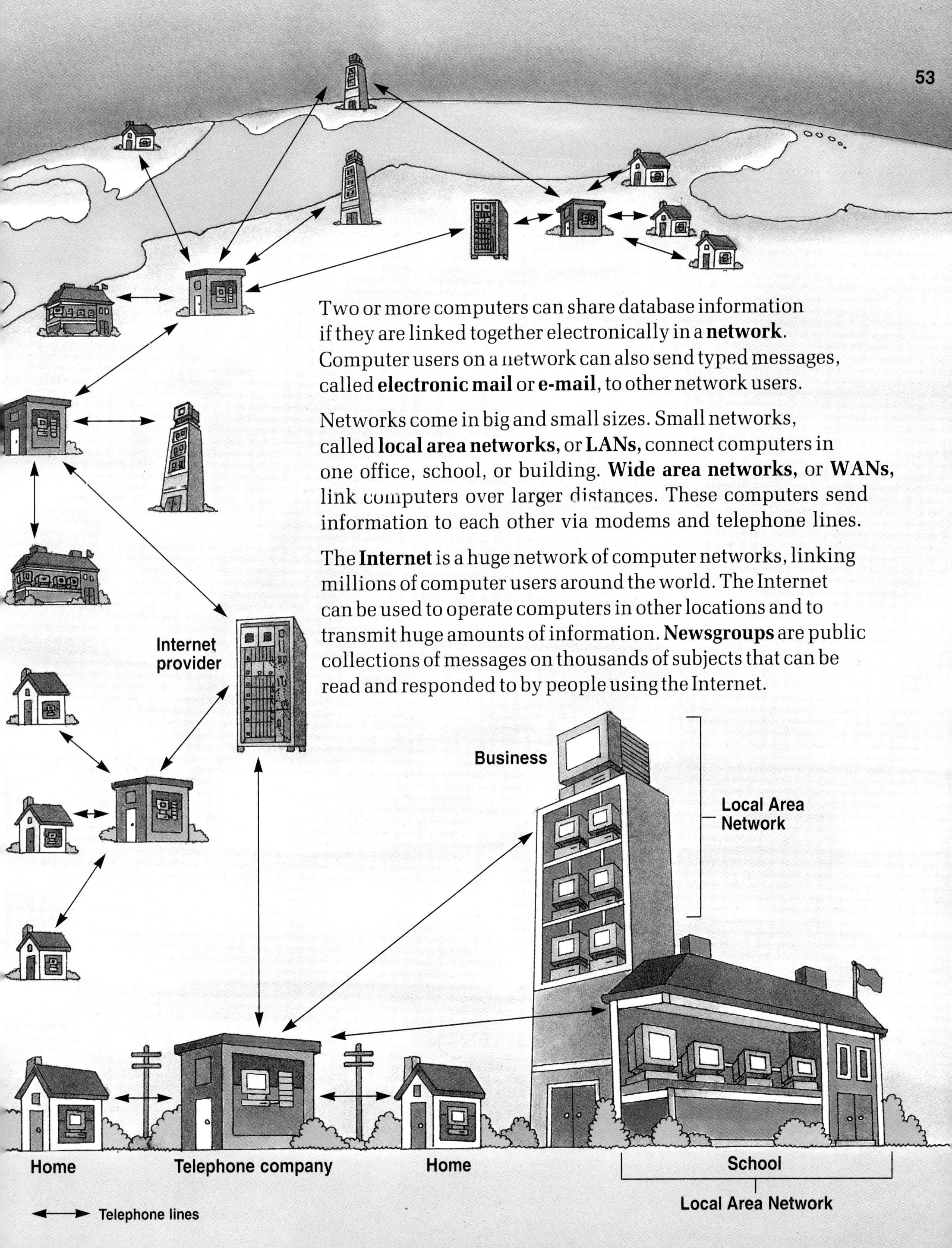

Two or more computers can share database information if they are linked together electronically in a **network**. Computer users on a network can also send typed messages, called **electronic mail** or **e-mail**, to other network users.

Networks come in big and small sizes. Small networks, called **local area networks**, or **LANs**, connect computers in one office, school, or building. **Wide area networks**, or **WANs**, link computers over larger distances. These computers send information to each other via modems and telephone lines.

The **Internet** is a huge network of computer networks, linking millions of computer users around the world. The Internet can be used to operate computers in other locations and to transmit huge amounts of information. **Newsgroups** are public collections of messages on thousands of subjects that can be read and responded to by people using the Internet.

Computer graphics

Look closely at a photograph in a newspaper or a magazine. You will see that the picture is made up of thousands of tiny dots. In the same way, a computer can display a picture made up of tiny points of light called **pixels** on a monitor screen. The more pixels, the better the quality of the picture.

Computer graphics is the name given to pictures and designs made with the help of a computer. The pictures in computer games are one example of computer graphics. Magazine artists create cover designs using computer graphics. Car designers use computer graphics to develop shapes for new cars. Computers help an architect to calculate and draw the plans for a new building. They can even show how the building would look from different angles. This use of computers is called **computer-aided design,** or CAD.

Graphic design software allows a person to create almost any kind of color image on the monitor. The image can be altered, copied, saved, or printed.

From television to virtual reality

Graphic design software allows an artist to create almost any kind of color image on the monitor. The image can be altered or copied, then saved on a disk and printed. Images can be made to look like paintings by adding simulated "brush strokes." Two photographic images can be combined into one to make a realistic but invented image that fools the eye. Repeated images can be used to create moving images, called **animations** (like cartoons). These animated images are often used for special effects in television and film.

This picture of a space city was drawn using a computer.

Animated graphics combined with sound and text are often used in educational and entertainment multimedia software on CD-ROM. Many multimedia programs are interactive, which means that the program responds to your input in a realistic, almost lifelike way. **Virtual reality (VR) technology** allows for even more realistic and lifelike interaction. With this technology you wear an electronic mask (called a **head-mounted display**) or electronic gloves wired with sensors (called **data gloves**), so that the computer can react to your eye and hand movements. You can explore a room, talk to other "people," and pick up objects that appear to be realistic and three-dimensional. None of these are real, however; they are all just images created by the computer.

Using a head-mounted display and data gloves, a person can experience a virtual world created by a computer and virtual reality technology.

Computers in flight

When an aircraft is flying, calculations have to be made all the time. These calculations tell the pilot how high he should be flying, the course he should be taking, how fast he should be going, and so on.

Today, these calculations are often done by computer. The planned altitude and course of the flight are fed into the flight deck computer before take-off. During the flight, sensors check the different parts of the aircraft. They produce electric signals which are processed and passed to the dials, screens, and lights in front of the pilot. Flashing lights and buzzers warn the pilot of any problems.

When an aircraft has reached the right altitude, a computer called an **autopilot** can take control. This computer uses all the flight information that was fed into it before take-off. It compares this information with what is actually happening in the aircraft. If the aircraft is not on exactly the right course, the autopilot can alter the controls. When the aircraft needs to land or if there is a problem such as bad weather, the crew take control again.

Pilots practice flying in the flight simulator of a computer-controlled aircraft. The simulator lets the pilots see what real flying will be like.

Controlling spacecraft

Computers are vital to space flight. Millions of calculations are needed to put a spacecraft into orbit and then return it to earth. On a space flight, computers at Mission Control constantly check the spacecraft's position, speed, and course. These data come by radio from the spacecraft. During the flight, fresh calculations are worked out at Mission Control and command signals are sent by radio to the spacecraft's equipment.

If the flight is unmanned, computers take complete control of the spacecraft. On a manned flight, the astronauts can work some of the controls themselves.

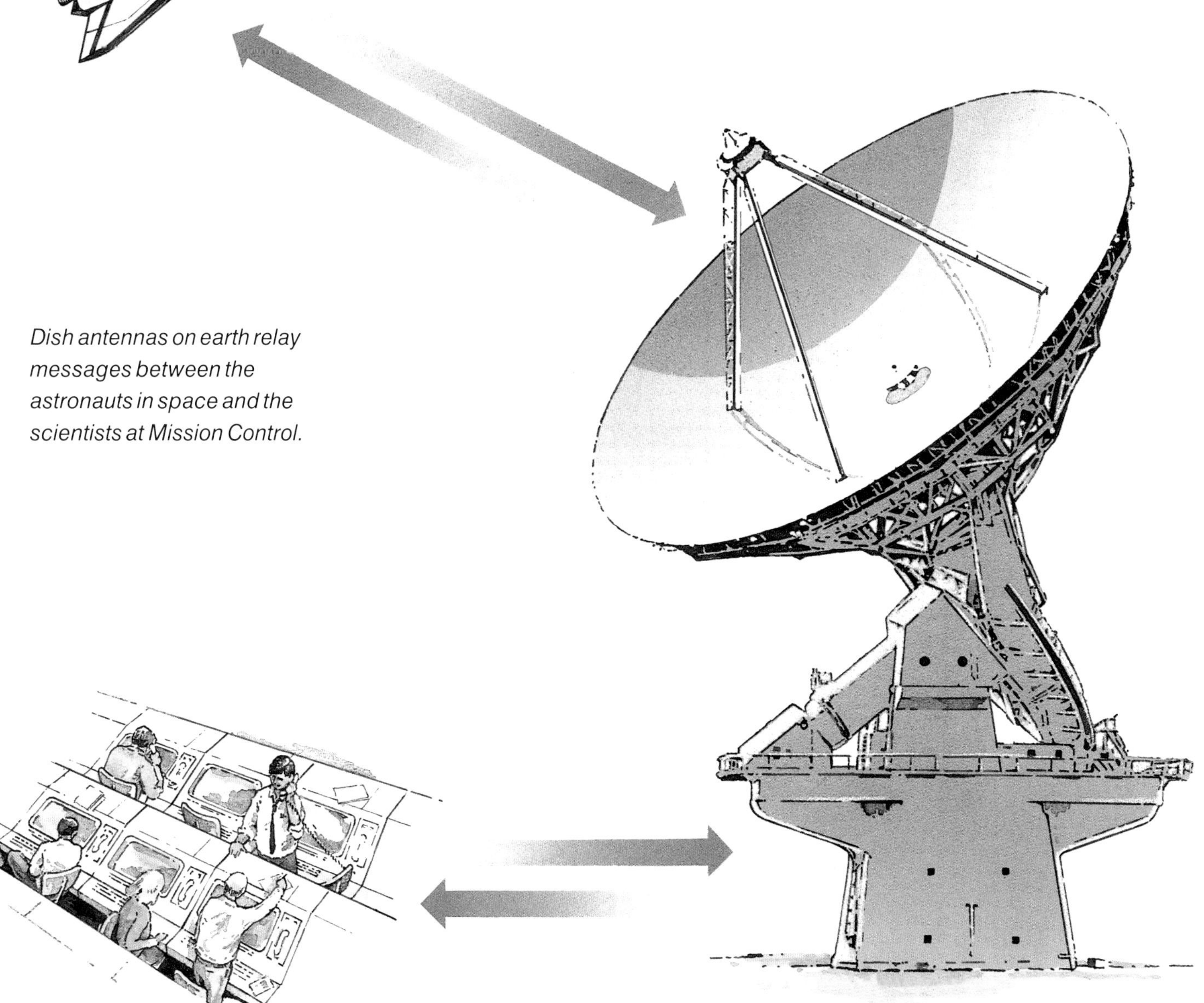

Dish antennas on earth relay messages between the astronauts in space and the scientists at Mission Control.

Robots at work

How would you like to spend all day putting the same metal pin into the same metal part over and over again? After a while, you would probably become tired or careless and start to do the job badly. Or how would you like to repair an oil pipeline at the bottom of an ocean? That job would be both difficult and dangerous. In modern industry, many of these tasks are performed by robots.

A **robot** is a machine that performs a task automatically. The robot's actions are controlled by a microprocessor that has been programmed for the task. A robot is different from a simple machine, because it can sense how well it is doing the job and can change its actions as needed. Scientists are using computer programs that imitate the human mind to develop "intelligent" robots that can perform complicated tasks in quickly changing situations.

Many industrial robots have metal arms with joints and complex metal "fingers" that can pick up small objects. In automobile factories, robots are used to assemble parts or weld them together, or to spray paint the car.

These robots are working on a car assembly line. They are connected to a computer that is programmed to control their movements.

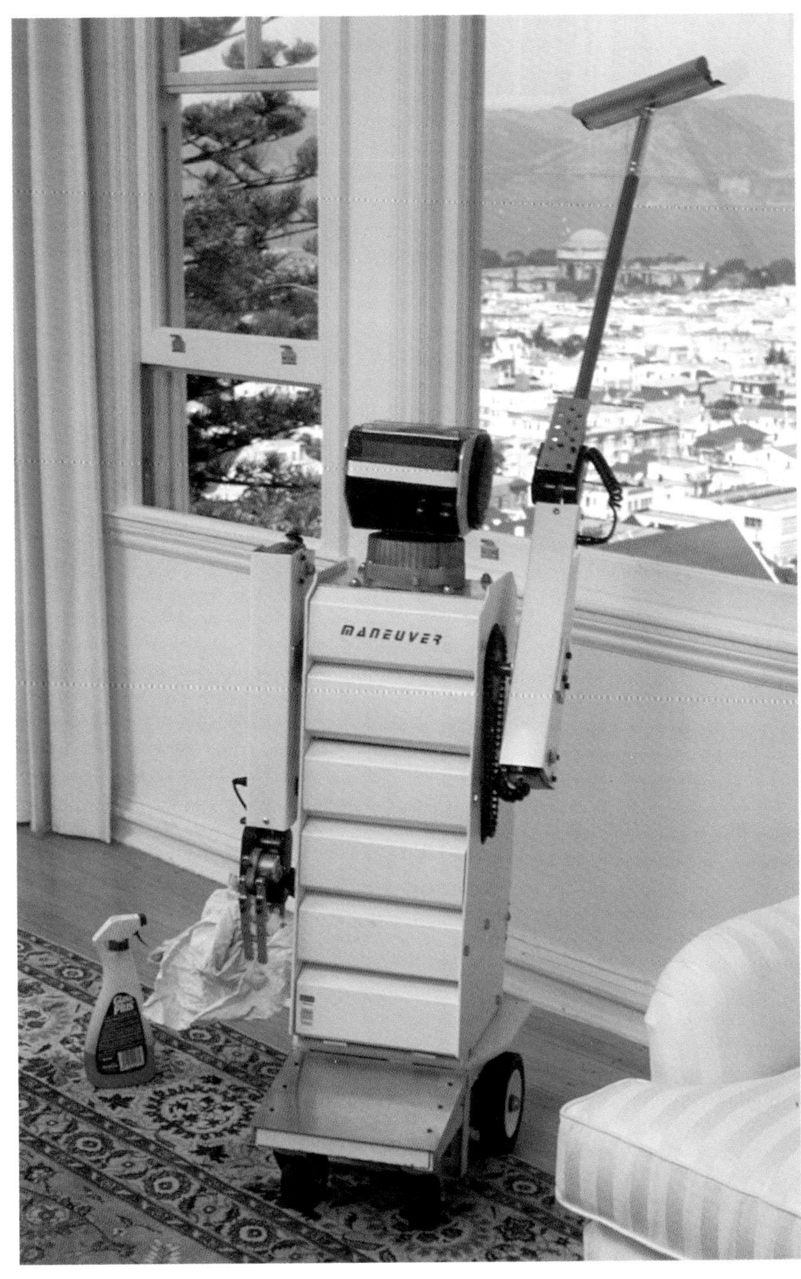

How would you like to program a robot to do your chores? This robot can clean windows, wash bathrooms, and make beds.

From strawberries to space

New robots are being invented to perform a wide variety of tasks. In farming, robots are used to pick strawberries. Robots in hospitals deliver food trays, medications, and lab supplies to nurses. Inventors of a snake like robot hope that it will be able to crawl through the rubble of collapsed buildings, searching for survivors. A robot with legs like a spider was used to explore an active volcano in Alaska.

Robots have been very useful in space exploration. Robots have explored both the moon and the planet Mars, testing soil, collecting samples, and sending images back to Earth.

A computer can beat you at chess, but that doesn't mean it's smarter than you are.

Can computers think?

Have you read or seen a science fiction story in which computers could do everything that humans can do? In real life, computers are not that clever, though they sometimes seem to be.

You can play chess with a computer, but you'll probably lose! This is not because the computer is more intelligent than you are. It's because the computer has been programmed to work out quickly every possible move on the chessboard, and what effect it will have on the game. If the computer is correctly programmed, it can't make a wrong move.

Artificial intelligence

Scientists are developing computers that seem to use intelligence to think. Most computers can only follow a strict set of instructions. **Artificial intelligence,** or AI, would make it possible for computers to learn new skills and to solve problems without any instructions. For example, artificial intelligence systems called **expert systems** can now indicate to doctors what diseases people have. Such systems need to be programmed with huge amounts of data before they can be used to solve the problems.

Some people believe that one day computers really will function like a human brain. Others think that situation is just science fiction. What do you think?

Glossary

Binary system, Base 2:
Counting system based on groups of two.

Bit:
One digit (either 0 or 1) in the binary system.

Bug:
Mistake in a *software program.*

Byte:
Eight bits, giving 256 combinations of 0 and 1. Each byte stands for a number, a letter, or other symbol.

CD-ROM, or Compact Disk Read-Only Memory:
A compact disk used to store computer data.

Chip:
Small piece of silicon on which a pattern is etched to form pathways for electric currents that carry out different tasks.

Computer:
Device that applies logic in performing rapid calculations.

Computer system:
All the parts needed to make a computer function. These include input and output devices as well as the parts housed in the computer itself.

Database:
Collection of information, or data, usually stored on a disk.

Disk drive:
Part of a computer that reads information from a disk or writes onto a *floppy* or *hard disk.*

Floppy disk:
Flat piece of magnetically coated plastic on which information can be stored electronically.

Hard disk:
Permanently installed disk that stores more information than a *floppy disk.*

Hardware:
Physical pieces of computer equipment.

Input:
Information fed into a computer.

Integrated circuit:
Group of electronic parts joined together in a protective case; a *chip.*

Internet:
A global *network* of computer networks.

Mainframe:
Large, powerful computer designed to be used at the same time by many users.

Memory:
Numbers, instructions, or other information held in reserve by a computer for later use.

Modem:
Device that sends and receives data on telephone lines between two computers.

Mouse:
Device used to control a pointer on the monitor screen.

Multimedia:
Software that uses more than one medium, such as sound, text, and animated graphics.

Network:
Two or more computers linked together electronically.

Output:
Answer or other result provided by a computer.

Printer:
Device that prints a hard copy of a computer's work.

Program:
Step-by-step directions written in a computer language that a computer follows to carry out a given task.

RAM, or Random Access Memory:
Computer memory that temporarily holds information the computer needs for a given task.

ROM, or Read-Only Memory:
Computer memory that holds essential information the computer needs to carry out any tasks.

Software:
Programs that can be used by the computer to perform different tasks.

Supercomputer:
The fastest and most powerful type of *mainframe* computer.

Virtual reality:
Computer system using hardware and software to create the illusion of moving in a three-dimensional computer-generated world.

Virus:
Software designed to damage or destroy data and *programs* on a computer.

Index